The Word Among Us

The Word Among Us

Reflections on the Readings of the Revised Common Lectionary

Year B Volume 2

Herbert O'Driscoll

Anglican Book Centre
Toronto, Canada

2000
Anglican Book Centre
600 Jarvis Street
Toronto, Ontario
M4Y 2J6

Anglican Book Centre Publishing is not affiliated with, and neither this nor any other of its publications is sponsored or endorsed by, The Word Among Us, Inc., Ijamsville, Maryland, U.S.A.

Cover illustration: Book of Hours, "The Temptation of Christ"

Canadian Cataloguing in Publication Data

O'Driscoll, Herbert, 1928-
   The word among us : reflections on the readings of the revised common lectionary

ISBN 1-55126-225-8 (Year B, v. 2)

1. Bible — Criticism, interpretation, etc. 2. Bible — Liturgical lessons, English. I. title.

BS511.5.037 1997   220.7   C97-932166-2

Contents

About This Book

I was struck recently by a remark made about preaching by Gerhardt Ebeling. He wrote, "Preaching is not so much God overhearing what we are saying to our people as it is our people overhearing what we are saying to God."

I regard those words as a reminder that, when we preach or teach, we reveal a great deal about ourselves, often far more than we think. The same is true of writing, but perhaps not to the same extent. Teaching or preaching makes us totally present to one another.

While this can be sobering — because in the humanity we share, all of us want to maintain at least some measure of privacy — it can also be encouraging. When we find ourselves wrestling with a text or a theme, and we discover that it is speaking to us, deeply challenging us, perhaps even moving and inspiring us, this is a good sign that the discussion or sermon we are preparing will speak to others. Our most effective preaching or teaching happens when our listeners know that we ourselves have been spoken to by what we are trying to set before them.

Very often in these pages I find myself chatting spontaneously about a passage because it has suddenly spoken to me, and I want to find the simplest and most immediate way of telling others — in this case, you the reader — what I have "heard." When we preach or teach in this way, there is something about the immediacy of it, as well as the personal vulnerability of it, that engages a listener.

By now you will have come to know what to expect in these pages. They are notes and reflections rather than ready-made lessons or homilies. I chose this way deliberately. Some who use these pages neither preach nor teach but are worshippers who wish to prepare for worship by reading something about the scriptures for a Sunday. I chose this way also because there is a mysterious power about the preaching event when it fully involves preacher and congregation.

All I have done is to offer possibilities. You, as Bible study leader or preacher, will choose your own path. You may, in fact, find a very different way from the one I have pointed out. The important thing is that the finished article is nothing less than your faith journey engaging the journeys of those who listen to you. May it always be true that in this engagement the Word of God is spoken and heard. Every blessing to your ministry.

Herbert O'Driscoll

First Sunday in Lent

Genesis 9:8–17
Psalm 25:1–9
1 Peter 3:18–22
Mark 1:9–15

Weavings

Common to all the readings is the theme of water as a way of God's establishing a covenant with us.

  In the first reading, water is the means whereby God cleanses the earth, bringing into being a covenant between God and all living things. In the second reading, water in the context of baptism is the way to a relationship with Jesus Christ. In the gospel, water, again in the context of baptism, is the way by which Jesus discerns his vocation and receives the Spirit of God. The psalmist sings of his trust in a God with whom he shares a covenant of mutual faithfulness.

Reflections

First Reading

The word *covenant* occurs with remarkable frequency in this passage.

> *I am establishing my covenant with you ...*
> *I establish my covenant with you, that never again ...*
> *This is the sign of the covenant ...*
> *[My bow] shall be a sign of the covenant ...*
> *I will remember my covenant ...*
> *I will remember ... the everlasting covenant ...*
> *This is the sign of the covenant ....*

The writer must have deemed it desperately important for his people to realize that they lived in a covenant with God.

Contemporary society seems not to have the least inkling of what it might mean to live in a covenant relationship with God. Yet, while our society as a whole does not use "God language" these days, perhaps the concept of covenant is not entirely absent.

I am inclined to see a sense of covenant developing in modern thought as we face certain realities that fill us with awe, and even fear. This is discernible particularly in our relationship with the planet as a living environment. The language we are using about our ecological concerns is more and more a language of covenant. For most modern people this covenant is understood as being made not with a transcendent God but with the planet itself. This passage of scripture reminds us that the covenant is not merely between God and humanity. God says to humanity that it is also *with every living creature that is with you, the birds, the domestic animals, and every animal of earth with you ...*, and this theme is repeated again and again.

Perhaps the massive reordering of the relationships of men and women in contemporary society is another sign of covenant being formed. Perhaps the new relationships that must grow among the great religions in this shrinking world are yet other signs of developing covenant. Are these and other reorderings of relationship at least harbingers of the possibility that our culture will once again be able to think in terms of living in a covenant relationship with a transcendent God?

The story of the covenant with Noah and his family shows how destruction can become redemption. The flood destroys a world, but from this destruction emerges a world that has a new relationship or covenant with God. Is it possible that the apparent destruction of old ways of doing things, including even traditional religious practices and understandings, is really the beginning of a new covenant? And should we be looking for the rainbow that is its sign?

The Psalm

Anyone who has experience of counselling knows that we talk of less intense things first, moving gradually to what we really need to share.

The psalmist speaks first of safe and unthreatening things: *my God, I put my trust in you ... teach me your paths.* There is a hint of other matters not easy to reveal: *let me not be humiliated.* Then we learn a little of his relationship with God, his certainty of God's *compassion and love, for they are ... everlasting.* But the tone changes again in the reference to *the sins of my youth.* Suddenly there is an intense appeal. *O Lord, forgive my sin, for it is great.*

We see here the great honesty of the psalms about human nature — the struggle to face the realities, the pretending, the defences that are set up before they all tumble down. We have all been through this before finally confessing the truth, even if it is only to ourselves.

The psalmist is reassured by his certainty of the covenant with God: *All the paths of the Lord are love and faithfulness to those who keep his covenant and his testimonies.* The same assurance is open to us, too.

Second Reading

We are listening to a voice teaching early Christians, perhaps a group of people about to be baptized. At that time the decision for baptism would have been a serious step to take, attended as it was by the possibility of persecution or even death. Nobody is being casual at this moment, neither the person speaking nor those listening to this portion of the apostle's letter being read.

The writer uses an image from the story of Noah and the ark in which the flood is made the means not merely of destruction but of salvation. People were *saved through water* and a new covenant established.

The writer and his readers or listeners are experiencing a kind of flood — a flood of threats, of persecution, of death. But this flood, even if it does its worst and sweeps them away, can also save them if they associate themselves and their suffering with that of their Lord. The new covenant of his death and resurrection can be theirs, sealed in baptism. Baptism becomes a mysterious journey of dying and rising, physically in the water in which they stand, spiritually in the ordeal they may have to bear.

This is a grim scripture. It assumes a situation most of us find difficult to imagine. However, in many parts of the world

Christian men and women see their baptism in such terms. In places like Rwanda, East Timor, and the Sudan, some have faced dangers and yet remained faithful, and some have died hoping for resurrection.

For all of us, life itself becomes a kind of flood that eventually bears us away. When this flood rises, whether in the form of pain or disease or time itself, we will find ourselves grasping at the kind of foundational statements of faith made here. We will seek assurance that *baptism ... now saves you ... through the resurrection of Jesus Christ, who has gone into heaven and is at the right hand of God.*

The Gospel

Once again we have images of water as a flood that both captures and releases, drowns and then spills a person out again ready for new living.

Jesus makes the big decision to associate himself with the new future-oriented movement of John. Pointing to a new and different future, John invites people to act out their commitment to a new human nature and a new kind of society by offering themselves to a momentary dying in the river's flow.

Jesus must have entered the waters with questions and doubts. He was closing a chapter of his life that seems to have been private and domestic and being drawn to a life of public ministry that was to be demanding, draining, dangerous, and eventually fatal. Notice the effect on our Lord of his entering the baptismal water.

1. *He saw the heavens torn apart and the Spirit descending like a dove on him.* In other words, Jesus perceives that there has been a major breakthrough in his life, and this realization gives him a deep sense of peace.

2. *A voice came from heaven, "You are my Son, the Beloved; with you I am well pleased."* Jesus feels himself to be addressed from beyond himself, and he understands this as an affirmation or approval of his search for a sense of who he is and what he is being called to do.

3. *The Spirit immediately drove him out into the wilderness.* So shattering has the experience of baptism been that Jesus knows he cannot continue with ordinary life at present. He must explore the deep meanings and consequences of his baptism. Above all, he has decisions to make.

Because, for many of us, baptism took place in remote childhood, it is not even a memory. Are we being told by this scripture that an adult Christian needs to recover a sense of the significance of the baptismal covenant?

In recent years the church has offered a way of renewing baptismal vows. This may be a way for us to experience at least some of what our Lord experienced standing in that river — a moment in which we can become aware of the presence of God in a piercing way; a moment when we have a sense of being addressed from beyond our pathetic and limited self; a moment when we seek some time, and maybe a place, to come to terms with this renewed covenant and, like our Lord in the wilderness, to make decisions about how we are going to live out our faith from now on.

Second Sunday in Lent

Genesis 17:1–7, 15–16
Psalm 22:23–30
Romans 4:13–25
Mark 8:31–38

Weavings

The theme of these readings is not an easy one to hear. We are being told that our relationship with God demands a great deal of trust.

In the first reading, Abraham is given a promise that seems utterly impossible of fulfilment. In the second reading, Paul recalls this moment in Abraham's life and says that the same quality of trust will be demanded of Christian faith. In the gospel, Jesus describes the cost of his vision of the kingdom of God, only to find that those around him cannot respond to the tremendous level of trust this vision calls for in those who pursue it. The theme of the psalmist is that God is indeed trustworthy.

Reflections

First Reading

The salient point of this scripture is that the storyteller is saying that at a very late stage in Abraham's life, a great change occurred that set a new direction for the remainder of his life.

This passage is saying to me that, if I am open to the possibility, I, too, may be called into a new relationship with God at any stage of life, even in my senior years. Few people realize this possibility and, therefore, do not expect to discover a renewal of faith and purpose late in life. Yet we sometimes see a person discovering new purpose and new health because they have been renewed spiritually and mentally.

I have a friend with many years of business experience whose life has been transformed by discovering that he has a call to pastoral visiting, especially to men of his own generation. He has accepted training to do this, and he daily grows and deepens in this ministry. I think of this friend when I hear God say to Abraham, *I will establish my covenant between me and you, and your offspring after you ... to be God to you and your offspring.* Through this ministry God drew my friend into covenant, and through his work the love of God has quietly and gently been communicated to many people. In this sense God has made my friend *the ancestor of a multitude.*

God says to Abram that his *name shall be Abraham,* and I see that this is also true of my friend. His name has not literally changed, but he has changed as a person because more has been revealed of the essential person he has always been.

There may be Abrahams and Sarahs in many people's experience — men and women who have been called into new covenant with God for some purpose that has opened up new possibilities in their own lives and has enriched other lives. Such people encourage all of us to risk ourselves in trusting God. If we are ready to risk trusting, we will find our trust borne out and the risk worthwhile.

The Psalm

Every great collection of art has within it those giant works that stand above the rest. For Shakespeare it may be *Hamlet*, for Michelangelo it may be the ceiling of the Sistine Chapel. Among the psalms this song stands out. There are few evocations of human desolation that equal it.

For a Christian the first line pierces deeply because we hear it on the lips of the crucified Christ: *My God, My God, why have you forsaken me?* Some maintain that he may have been turning to this psalm to find some meaning in the agony of crucifixion; but as we know, the psalm is not about the crucifixion of our Lord. The psalmist is writing from some personal agony that has been going on for some time: *I cry in the daytime, but you do not answer; by night as well, but I find no rest.* He tries the devices we all know in suffering. God has helped in the past; therefore, surely help can be expected now: *Our forebears put their trust in you ... and you delivered them.* For a moment this gives relief, but then he recalls the contempt received from others: *All who see me laugh me to scorn.*

One of the cruel consequences of great suffering is the thought that we are worthless and have become of no consequence even to friends: *I am a worm and no man, scorned ... despised.* Once again the psalmist makes an effort to regain control of his feelings. After all, God is the creator. Surely this suffering is of concern to the maker of one's body and soul: *You are he who took me out of the womb.* But the effort at control is swept away in a sudden flood of misery. *I am poured out like water; all my bones are out of joint; my heart ... is melting wax ... My mouth is dried out ... Packs of dogs close me in ... gangs of evildoers circle around me.*

Now a change begins. *I will declare your name to my brethren; in the ... congregation I will praise you ... I will perform my vows ...* There is a stiffening of resolve, a gathering of personal resources based on trust in God. God does not *hide his face ... but when they cry to him he hears them.*

Now it seems that the sufferer has succeeded in handing over his suffering to greater hands, *For kingship belongs to the Lord.* We hear the voice of someone who is preparing for final surrender: *To him alone all who sleep in the earth bow down in worship.* But then suddenly we hear, *My soul shall live for him.* A sense of the future floods in: *my descendants shall serve him; they shall be known as the Lord's for ever.*

We have been given a sublime expression of the determination of the human spirit to find in God meaning and hope, even in suffering.

Second Reading

Once again we hear of Abraham as Paul writes to the community in Rome. Abraham is an example of something that is central to Paul's own Christian faith and to the form in which he presents it to these early Christian communities. Abraham's relationship with God was founded on, and flourished through, his faith in God's promises. Such trust was by no means easy. There were times when he realized that, because of his own great age, the promises were unlikely ever to come to reality. Sometimes he was overcome by doubts and fears, yet *no distrust made him waver ... but he grew strong in his faith ... being fully convinced that God was able to do what he had promised.*

Paul offers Abraham's story as a pattern for his listeners and for us. If the faith and trust of Abraham were the foundation of the magnificent relationship between Abraham and God, then faith and trust can also be the means of forming our relationship with God. For us as Christians, our way to God is through Jesus Christ, who has died and risen. To place our confidence in this suffering and risen Lord is to find ourselves in relationship with God.

The Gospel

This was not the first time Jesus had tried to get his disciples to see the shadows looming in their future work together, but as always, the effort failed. What our Lord must have felt when the utterly dependable Peter — the one he had affectionately called the Rock — came to him asking that he stop talking in this way, we can only imagine. However, the gospel writer makes one aspect of Jesus' response very obvious — Jesus was appalled and enraged. It would have been impossible for Peter not to have been deeply distressed by the awful name of Satan hurled at him by his leader and friend. If ever there was a moment in their relationship that might have broken the bond between them, this was it. But Peter's trust held, and so the bond between them held.

[Jesus] called the crowd with his disciples. I hear Jesus despairing of getting anyone to understand the cost of following him. In this outburst he is again repeating this single theme, trying to find the perfect expression of it that will at last pierce through to his listeners.

If any want to become my followers, let them deny themselves. To be associated with him, to follow him, to share the dream of his kingdom, means self-sacrifice. One wonders what is going on in the minds of the disciples as they listen. Could this really be the person who so attracted them on the lakeshore when it all started? If being Christian must always demand self-sacrifice, then do we ourselves have some rethinking to do?

Those who want to save their life will lose it, and those who lose their life for my sake ... will save it. The power of this statement, and the reason why it will always haunt us, lies in its eluding all our efforts to define it. I think that the word *life* in this statement means life that is fully committed to something other than the self. To live fully committed to the self means trying to save oneself, in the sense of preserving oneself, guarding oneself, keeping control of life. To live fully committed to something other than the self means giving oneself completely to this other reality. In a sense it means throwing our lives into it — some would say it means throwing our lives away. But this is exactly what our Lord seems to be saying. Only those who take the risk — who trust enough to throw their lives into a vision that may to some look lunatic — will truly and fully find what their lives are about. In other words, they will save their lives.

Jesus chooses another way to reach any who will listen. What will it profit them to gain the whole world and forfeit their life? Again, it is quite possible to save our life by centring our energies on the self and taking no risks. In other words, we can choose to live safely. But when we choose this road, we often find that we have mysteriously lost something, and there can be real sadness.

These words of our Lord are haunting, elusive, poetic. We can never probe them fully, but we know with absolute certainty that they contain an immense truth about life and the choices we make or refuse to make.

Third Sunday in Lent

Exodus 20:1–17
Psalm 19
1 Corinthians 1:18–25
John 2:13–22

Weavings

In the sequence of these readings we are confronted by four great realities: in the first reading and the psalm, the Jewish law, first given on Sinai; in the second reading, the greatness of Greek wisdom or philosophy; in the gospel, the magnificent cultic life of the Temple in Jerusalem, and in both second reading and gospel, the Passion of our Lord Jesus Christ. As we read, we are shown their relationship.

Reflections

First Reading

There was a time when it was taken for granted that every Christian knew this passage by heart. Even in my own lifetime there echoes the admonition at baptism that "this child be taught the

Creed, the Ten Commandments and the Lord's Prayer, and be further instructed in the Church Catechism, and then be brought to the Bishop to be confirmed." These were the conditions of my own confirmation. But things have greatly changed. Learning by heart is no longer in favour. I am quite certain that it will one day return as a fascinating and exciting new idea in educational circles — but we must wait and see.

A corollary flows from all this. It is easy to forget that these commandments are very largely unfamiliar to a new generation, and by "new generation" I do not mean only children.

But there are other reasons why this scripture is out of favour. We no longer like a God who gives stern directives. Our prime requirement of God is that he/she be loving. There is nothing wrong with this as long as we remember that sometimes love — even on a human level — means a measure of sternness and discipline. When God says, *I am the Lord your God,* the words are far more than a mere helpful identifying of the speaker. They are heavy with authority. They invite attention. If we are wise, we do not expect a cosy chat with a kind of invisible but easygoing colleague. We are being invited to bow down and to obey, neither of which activities is very popular these days.

Perhaps our culture needs to pay particular attention to the second commandment: *You shall not make for yourself an idol.* The word *idol* here does not mean the kind of figure we might expect to come across in an Indiana Jones movie. It means anything — anything whatsoever — that we put in place of God as the paramount reality in our lives. We spend millions of dollars constructing idols. Only recently I heard the new slogan for Volvo automobiles: "a car that can save your soul." In both business and government, there is a tendency to assess all social bonds and human needs on a monetary scale alone.

Some would claim that certain adopted attitudes of our culture have become idols, among them some kinds of feminism and political correctness. To say this is not for a moment to wish to extirpate either. Feminism released into our culture the gifts and energies of half the human race. Political correctness has shown the power of language to hurt or to heal, even to bring realities into being. But when such a powerful new force becomes the ultimate criterion for judging everything else — even sometimes the gospel itself — we must remind ourselves that all gifts of God can be fashioned into idols.

The Psalm

In this wonderful and ancient song, the glory of the sun and the glory of God's law become mirrored in each other. Both embody the divine perfection. *The heavens declare the glory of God ... The law of the Lord is perfect.* Both possess a certainty, an utter dependability. *The sun ... goes forth from the uttermost edge of the heavens ... to the end of it again ... the judgements of the Lord are true and righteous altogether.* Both are a source of joy in life. *The sun ... rejoices like a champion to run its course ... The statutes of the Lord are just and rejoice the heart.* As the sun is the source of light, so *the commandment of the Lord is clear and gives light to the eyes.* All of the vast created order, the environment and nourishment for our living, expresses the life and joy and glory of God.

In verses 7–11 we hear a voice singing of a source of grace in human experience that is beyond that experience itself. The law of God gives grace in various ways. It *revives the soul ... gives wisdom ... rejoices the heart ... gives light to the eyes.* To those who possess it, *there is great reward.* For a Christian reading this psalm, these properties of the Law may be seen as gifts that flow to us from our Lord. He is our Torah. He is the source that revives our souls, offers wisdom, provides light for our way.

To know him and to follow him is to receive a great reward. Above all, it is through our Lord that *"he words of my mouth and the meditation of my heart be acceptable in [God's] sight.*

Second Reading

It is difficult for us to realize the degree to which Christian faith challenged almost everything that people took for granted in those early societies. If you were a Jew, then someone who had been crucified was among the lowest of the low. If you were Greek, then a movement that seemed to care nothing for the intellectual world of Greek philosophy could hold no significance. Paul understood all this. He himself was completely at home in both worlds. This is what he is saying explicitly in the opening words of this passage: *The message about the cross is foolishness to those who are perishing.* In every generation there have been those who have dismissed Christian faith as nonsense. Very often it is the intellectuals and the elites of society who have the greatest difficulty with the faith.

Paul tackles the problem head on. He does not defend a position; rather he attacks. He presents our Lord, his passion and his resurrection as a direct challenge to human intellect. For Paul the ultimate value lies beyond intellect in faith or trust. This is not to say that Paul scorns intellect. There are many times when he debates with both systems of thought: Jewish Law and Greek philosophy. But he maintains that the heart of the matter lies beyond them both.

Yes, Christian faith maintains that Jesus shows little interest in either system. Yes, Christian faith shows that Jesus refuses to exercise power as the world knows it. Yes, Christian faith sees Jesus caught in the utter degradation of crucifixion. Yes, Christian faith proclaims that Jesus Christ lives after that terrible death. Yes, every one of these things collides with what most people regard as normal and understandable. But, Paul seems to say,

Can you not see that it is in this very challenge to all that seems normal and reasonable and sensible that the truth lies? It is not that Jewish law or Greek philosophy — or any of our modern or post modern systems of thought — are of no account. But God has deliberately stepped far beyond them in Jesus Christ.

Is this foolish of God? If so, says Paul, *God's foolishness is wiser than human wisdom, and God's weakness is stronger than human strength.*

The Gospel

We do not know if this was the first time that Jesus stood in the great outer court of the Temple as an adult. We know that he was here as a child in arms, and twelve years later as a youth. Now he surveys the scene through adult eyes.

This vast courtyard was one of the meeting places of the ancient world. In those days there were about three million Jews in the country and about four million spread across the Mediterranean world. Anyone who could possibly afford to come to the Temple did so. As soon as a visitor climbed the vast steps and entered the courtyard, he had to buy something to make a sacrifice. Prices were high, and the only money that was accepted was the local currency, the shekel. Every visitor had to change money. The rates were exorbitant. The treasury of the Temple was one of the ancient world's great banking houses.

In this scene, Jesus is disgusted. Disgust turns to anger, and anger turns to action. Obviously he makes quite a disturbance.

He is not dismissing the worship of the Temple. He is not attacking the spiritual tradition that has formed his whole life and will remain in the hearts of the first generation of his own followers as long as they live in or near Jerusalem. He is attacking the perversion of this ancient and glorious tradition: *Stop making my Father's house a marketplace!* For Jesus this is a sacred place, the dwelling place of God. The Jews who gather around him and ask, *What sign can you show us for doing this?* may themselves have reservations about the uses to which the Temple precincts are being put.

Now comes the play on the word *temple* when, John tells us, Jesus speaks of his own resurrection. John is saying to the first readers of his gospel that there is a reality greater than the Temple and its spiritual tradition. This greater reality is embodied in Jesus Christ, crucified and risen.

John is also saying something to those of us who read his gospel today. It is the theme in all today's readings. Beyond all religious systems — both Paul and John tell us — stands Jesus. He is nothing less than the judge of all systems, even a Christian system! There may be Christian faith, Christian churches, Christian philosophy, Christian ethics, Christian social thought. All of these things have their value, but all are under the judgement of the One who is born, suffers, dies, and rises to bring them into being.

Fourth Sunday in Lent

Numbers 21:4–9
Psalm 107:1–3, 17–22
Ephesians 2:1–10
John 3:14–21

Weavings

In each of the readings God enters the human situation to heal in some way.

In the first reading and the psalm, it is Israel, either in the wilderness or in exile, that needs and receives healing. In the second reading, those Greco-Roman citizens who have been called into the Christian faith find it to be for their healing. In the gospel, the whole of humanity is offered our Lord Jesus Christ as healing. The scope of God's healing broadens and spreads as we move through this sequence of scripture.

Reflections

First Reading

They set out ... but the people became impatient on the way.
This image of a fractious and discontented caravan speaks to
me about Christian faith today. We are very divided, with a vast
number of conflicting schools of thought, opinions, convictions
— or prejudices, depending on who is making the judgement!
We are convinced that this is an age of crisis for the church and
for Christian faith. We are involved in endless arguments as to
who exactly Jesus was and is. In all this we are tempted to imagine that there have been great past ages of faith and consensus
and unity, when Christian faith was strong and spiritual giants
roamed the land.

I suspect that the truth is rather different. To some extent
every generation of Christian faith has felt itself to be on a wilderness journey. Every generation has had its grumbles and its
disagreements within congregations and with leadership. Every
generation has been constantly engaged in the reinterpretation
of Christian faith.

The seething impatience of those people in the wilderness
long ago shows in their dissatisfaction with leadership and their
resentment at the demands being made upon them and at the
effort necessary for the journey. We can hear their complaining
across the centuries. *Why have you brought us up ... out of
Egypt to die in the wilderness? ... we detest this miserable food.*
Their general discontent focuses on the very basic matter of
food, just as our discontent, in churches and congregations, at work
or at home or in voluntary activities, often finds its focus in some
outwardly minor issue around which everything else gathers.

Something ugly and frightening happens. They encounter
an infestation of poisonous snakes local to the region. Some

people are bitten and they die. This is immediately seen as a judgement on their grumbling. For people of their time and culture this is a perfectly reasonable assumption to make. Disaster has come. There must be some reason for it. They seek the reason in their own behaviour. *We have sinned,* they say to Moses. Whether we see it their way or not should not blind us to a lesson we can learn. These ancient people were much better prepared than we to take responsibility for unfavourable events. We tend to attribute responsibility for unfavourable events to anything but our own behaviour!

Moses made a serpent of bronze, and put it upon a pole. The image of the snake was a widespread and ancient symbol of healing. The *caduceus* symbol, a wand with two serpents twined around it, is still used by the medical profession today. Given the deep trust in such a symbol and the instinctive linking of symbol and reality characteristic of ancient times, it is possible that the very sight of the symbol was strongly therapeutic and assisted in the struggle for life in spite of the poison.

The Psalm

These verses closely echo the content of the lesson. They begin with a categorical statement about the nature of God. To these people, in spite of all they have been through, *[God] is good and his mercy endures for ever.* Again, a link is made between some things that happen to them and their own actions: *Some ... were afflicted because of their sins.* We are loath to use such direct language because we do not wish to be judgemental, yet the connection between sin and suffering remains, in spite of our reluctance to make what we coyly call value judgements.

They cried to the Lord in their trouble, and he delivered them from their distress. He sent forth his word and healed them and saved them from the grave. I have always felt that these verses are a magnificent tribute to the resilience of Jewish faith down through the centuries — centuries of persecution and wandering when *they cried to the Lord in their trouble* but still sang the song of thanksgiving to a saving, healing, and loving God. When we hear them *give thanks to the Lord for his mercy and the wonders that he does for his children,* telling *of his acts with shouts of joy,* we bow our heads with shame for the unthinking ingratitude we ourselves sometimes indulge in.

Second Reading

The language Paul uses to describe the mental and spiritual world in which people lived is very powerful. It gets across the extraordinary way that a culture can capture minds in any age. When Paul refers to *the ruler of the power of the air, the spirit that is now at work,* we can understand his words to suggest the massive forces that bear on society today, among them the media that form minds, create attitudes, invent desires, dictate fashions, make themselves the arbitrars of thought, and define with a kind of arrogant authority what is and is not politically correct.

Paul speaks of living *in the passions of our flesh, following the desires of flesh and senses.* The word *flesh* in Paul's letters does not merely mean our bodies. It means life lived utterly for the self, for personal wants and desires, and with no reference beyond the self. It involves sensuality but goes further to include a total way of life — what we now call a *lifestyle.* It is precisely this lifestyle from which Christ can release us. It is not a matter of our deserving anything. It is not a matter of our having to reach some moral plateau where we become acceptable to receive this grace. As Paul says, *This is not your own doing.* It is there for the asking and receiving. To receive this grace is to recognize it as a gift of God.

What does it mean to receive the grace of Jesus Christ? I think Paul gives us a clue when he says, *For we are what he has made us, created in Christ Jesus for good works.* I think I hear Paul saying something like this to us in our own culture:

You and I are not made to be the pawns of forces that try to mould both society and the person for their own use. We are not created to be merely consumers. We have only to think a little about the term *consumer* to realize the extraordinary insult it contains — endlessly unsatisfied, only voracious appetites totally centred on the self and its demands. You and I were created by God for a very different purpose. God has made us to reflect what we see in Jesus Christ, a being not centred on the self but on good works. This is the way of life we are offered. When we accept it, we become who we really are and were created to be — members of the body of Jesus Christ.

The Gospel

John gives us the words spoken by our Lord himself, thus making the image of the serpent more poignant. Jesus recalls the wilderness incident when the bronze serpent was fashioned and lifted for all to see, giving many healing. Jesus sees himself as the healing serpent, raised by the obscene act of crucifixion, yet giving healing to those who look.

I suddenly realize that among the many images we have of Jesus — good shepherd, light of the world, and so on — I have never heard this image mentioned. It depicts utter opposites — the serpent in the garden at the beginning of creation, and the serpent on the cross in an act of new creation. One seeks to manipulate and corrupt our human nature; the other, to free us and save our human nature. One appeals to our selfish desires; the other, to the very highest in us. One seduces, the other loves. One brings about our banishment from the presence of God, the other draws us into the presence of God. There is a host of rich meanings in this image of the two serpents — Satan, the serpent of temptation; Jesus, the serpent of salvation.

All of today's readings point to God as the source of healing for our humanity. This source of healing is offered as a focus of our contemplation. In the first reading, contemplating the bronze serpent — the symbol of God as healer — can bring healing. In the second reading, contemplating Jesus can release us from the seduction of self and make us what we were created by God to be — beings whose truest role is to exist for others: *he has made us ... for good works*. In the gospel, contemplating our Lord on the cross draws us from the darkness of self-centredness to the light of serving him and living in his name.

Fifth Sunday in Lent

Jeremiah 31:31–34
Psalm 51:1–13
Hebrews 5:5–10
John 12:20–33

Weavings

As we would expect at this time when our Lord's passion draws near, the prospect of death , and in particular the significance of our Lord's death, hangs over all of these readings.

The first reading begins by speaking of a new covenant. As Christians, we know that a new covenant will be made by our Lord's death. The psalm tells us that the covenant God really wishes is made within the human heart. The second reading speaks of a high priest. As Christians, we know that Jesus will become a high priest by sacrificing himself on the cross. In the gospel, Jesus receives people who have come a long way to see him. Then he envisions a world coming to see him as he hangs on a cross.

Reflections

First Reading

The days are surely coming, says the Lord, when I will make a new covenant. Heard through Christian ears, this statement is full of meaning — meaning that includes sadness, even dread. The Christian reader knows the awful cost of making the new covenant, to be celebrated in the liturgies of this season. The maker of the covenant with our humanity is God, but it is our Lord Jesus Christ, in his death and resurrection, who becomes the means by which this new covenant is made.

For present–day readers much of this is hard to fathom. The concept of covenant as it is understood in the Bible has almost vanished from contemporary awareness. Let us try to begin not at the beginning, but with our Lord.

Imagine that you are standing on that ghastly hill looking at Jesus of Nazareth die. Two other people are dying just as horribly. Living in Palestine two millennia ago, you would have seen crosses with bodies on them as often as someone living in eighteenth-century England would have seen bodies hanging from gibbets at crossroads. What is special about the dying man on the centre cross?

If we believe what Christian faith says about this man — that in him God is present in human form in a unique way — then something extraordinary has happened to the human nature we all share. For the last thirty years or so it has, in this person, been lived in perfect obedience to God. This is something none of the rest of us can do. In us there is a battle between our own will and God's will. In Jesus there certainly was a human will, but it was totally offered to doing God's will.

Jesus has taken human life, lived it in perfect obedience, then offered it back to God. In this one life the bond between

God and humanity — normally fragile in all our lives — is rock-solid once again. The Bible's way of expressing this is to say that in Jesus a covenant has been made between God and humanity.

We should really say that this covenant has been *remade*, because God has tried again and again to make it before. This passage from Jeremiah refers to the making of a covenant with Israel, as they came out of Egypt long ago. God still makes covenant with us today, and we break it. Yet God, loving and forgiving, always tries again. Almost always in the stories of remaking the covenant, we get an image of God as the lover of humanity. In this particular passage God is referred to as the *husband* of our human nature.

In this passage God seems to be saying that the next making of covenant will be within the hearts of people. Traditionally religion among the people of God had been predominantly external — the saying of ritual words, the carrying out of ritual acts. This time it will be different, the prophet says. He seems to visualize a future where the faith of the people will be not so much an institutionally formalized religion as a personally experienced spirituality that somehow spreads spontaneously: *I will put my law within them, and I will write it on their hearts.*

Perhaps we are seeing something of this kind of thing in our own day. Interest in institutional religion is generally at a low ebb, yet there is an immense tide of spirituality flowing in the culture. This spiritual tide has many currents — not to speak of a great deal of flotsam and jetsam floating on its surface — but it is nevertheless powerful and significant.

The Psalm

The psalm repeatedly echoes Jeremiah's concept of the new covenant — a covenant of the inner life, a kind of new spiritual questing.

We hear these echoes first as the psalmist realizes that his own sinfulness is an internal thing. He also acknowledges that God requires not external responses, but *truth deep within me.* If inner integrity is present, then the external actions that follow will have their own integrity. Therefore he asks God to help him *understand wisdom secretly.*

Three times more we hear him speak of his relationship with God as essentially an interior one. He prays, *Create in me a clean heart, O God,* and offers his spirit for transforming into *a right spirit.* He realizes that these things can exist only if the Holy Spirit of God is within him in the first place: *take not your holy Spirit from me.*

Second Reading

When the early Christians began to think about the meaning of the extraordinary encounter with Jesus — his words, his actions, his death, his resurrection — they sought many ways of giving it meaning. One way was to link it to things familiar from their former experience as Jews.

Every year the high priest of Israel went alone into the Holy of Holies in the Temple to offer sacrifice for the sins of the whole people of God. It was understood that by this sacrifice the bond with God, broken by human sin, was forged once again for at least another year.

This tradition was used by the Christians to explain what Jesus had done. He, too, had gone into the ultimate Holy of Holies. He had gone through death into the presence of God. There he offered to God a sacrifice, this time for the whole of humanity. The sacrifice he offered was nothing less than himself, and the bond he forged between humanity and God would remain forever.

The cost of that terrible sacrifice is mentioned here. The writer points to Jesus' terror before the ordeal. *Jesus offered up prayers and supplications, with loud cries and tears.* The writer makes no attempt to hide the humanity of our Lord at this time in his life. Jesus behaves in an utterly human way, but it is by the offering of himself totally to God that *he became the source of eternal salvation for all who obey him.* In other words (as simply as I dare to put this profound truth), if as a Christian I deliberately associate myself with Jesus and commit myself to his way of living out my human nature — that is, *obey him* — then he becomes my salvation.

But what do I mean when I say that he becomes my salvation? If I commit myself to Jesus' way of living my human nature, I am saved from the foolishness and the loss of trying to live to myself alone.

The Gospel

I have always found this moment in the gospel deeply moving. I see it taking place under lowering skies, the quickly changing, late-winter, early-spring skies one sees in the Jerusalem area. I see our Lord weary, dispirited, even morose.

I am intrigued that the Greek visitors came to Philip. I wonder if Philip had a naturally welcoming stance. I wonder, too, why Philip first went to Andrew. Was Philip a bit diffident in the presence of Jesus? Did he need an ally to make a request? Or does Philip's hesitation in making the request on his own suggest that there was something about Jesus' mood and manner that made them hesitate to bring this further demand to his attention?

Jesus' reply is indirect, oblique, dark. It must have had a chilling effect on the two disciples. *Unless a grain of wheat falls into the earth and dies, it remains just a single grain; but if it dies, it bears much fruit.* It is just possible that this statement could have been made with excitement and a kind of grim satisfaction. Jesus seems to be saying that, in this wish of the

Greek visitors to see him, he perceives the first signs of the spread of the kingdom into far places. But he leaves his disciples with no illusions about the cost of reaching those far places. To grow, the seed must die. The cost will be his own death.

Jesus readily acknowledges that his *soul is troubled.* There is a foreboding of future terror: *it is for this reason that I have come to this hour.* He seems momentarily to forget the presence of his disciples. Perhaps he leaves them, walks a little from them, and gazes into the distance, as if searching for another companionship that may respond to his terrible need. *Father, save me from this hour.*

He receives a response. A change of expression, a straightening of the body, a look in his eyes suggests to the watching crowd that a response has been given. In their ears they hear a rumble of thunder.

The response changes Jesus. Suddenly he is sure and certain, as if he sees a way ahead that formerly was hidden. *Now the ruler of this world will be driven out.* The dark mood lifts. Passivity changes to assertion. *And I, when I am lifted up from the earth, will draw all people to myself.* Even though spoken quietly, his words ring with authority. As he says them, I wonder if he is looking at the group of Greek visitors, looking at them and yet beyond them, seeing an unimaginable host of those who will be drawn to him in the centuries ahead — among them you and me.

Passion/Palm Sunday

Mark 11:1–11
Isaiah 50:4–9a
Psalm 31:9–16
Philippians 2:5–11
Mark 14:1—15: 47

Weavings

Today's scriptures offer great riches. The Mark passage for the liturgy of the palms is a story in itself. The Isaiah passage can be read as expressing the thoughts of our Lord as he decides to confront the forces arrayed against him. The psalm echoes these thoughts and shows how a strong trust in God is necessary in such a confrontation. The Philippians passage continues to offer insight into the inner motivation of our Lord. The gospel takes us into the full sweep of the events that lead to the terrible hilltop of Calvary.

Reflections

The Liturgy of the Palms

The Gospel

We are on the eastern slope of the Mount of Olives. The city lies over the brow of the mountain, still out of view and well beyond the two small villages named here, Bethphage and Bethany. We have the sense that the die is cast only when Jesus goes over the brow of the mountain and faces the city.

The colt has been secured by some previous arrangement. There is even an arranged signal. Someone will ask, *Why are you doing this?* and the two disciples are to reply, *The Lord needs it and will send it back here immediately.* If indeed this does point to a secret arrangement, it shows the degree to which our Lord felt himself under surveillance even before the events of these terrible days began.

Almost as if there is a spontaneous understanding of his purpose, the procession gathers and begins to climb the steep hillside to the brow of the mountain. This symbolic action speaks to the people about things they have known since childhood. Some day, the old story went, a person will ride to Zion on a beast such as this, claiming authority in Israel. Suddenly they are seeing this story come alive in front of them. They know their role. They must support what Jesus is doing. Quite possibly, some of them have visions of the next few hours precipitating a massive revolution that will change their society and its history.

On they go, working their way down to the Kidron valley, crossing it, and beginning the climb towards the edge of the city, through one of the gates, and along the narrow streets into the Temple area. Jesus dismounts and climbs the steps at the south end of the vast Temple complex. He probably goes no farther than the entrance to the great court of the Gentiles. For some time he stands there, watching the ceaseless activity of the huge cosmopolitan crowd, then turns to rejoin those who have come thus far with him. He may or may not have spoken to the crowd. It would seem that they have dispersed. As evening falls he and the twelve — even Judas is participating in this event — set out to walk back to Bethany. Most likely there is a bed there for him in the house of Mary, Martha, and Lazarus. For the others, there will be billets with friends or extended family.

We could think of the city as the vast interwoven systems of our own day — commercial, cultural, financial, political. Into this world of work and tension and creativity and achievement our Lord comes, claiming moral authority, asking uncomfortable questions. What replies do we give? What is our response to his claim?

We could also think of the city as the human soul, our own soul. Into this little city our Lord also comes. Once again he comes as one with authority. To what extent do we accept this authority? To what extent do we obey it?

This entry into the city is the first scene in the story that continues in the scriptures and liturgies of the next few days.

The Liturgy of the Passion

First Reading

Although this passage was written many centuries before the earthly life of our Lord, it is used here as a kind of parallel expression of what may have been going on in his thoughts.

The writer begins by expressing satisfaction in his vocation and its gifts. He loves teaching and he loves the way that he is able to *sustain the weary with a word.* But for reasons we cannot know, this role has been very costly. He has made enemies. We hear him say, *I did not hide my face from insult and spitting.*

Even in the face of this he will not relent from carrying out his purpose. He challenges all who would wish to stop him and even harm him. He knows his enemies, but he also knows where his own strength comes from. *It is the Lord God who helps me.*

We can easily see how this reading may anticipate the thoughts of our Lord as he faces this last week. He, too, has taught the things of the kingdom of God. He, too, has suffered for that activity. He, too, refuses to be turned back from his purpose. He, too, turns to God as his source of strength for what lies ahead.

The Psalm

These lines continue to parallel our Lord's experience. For the psalmist there is *sorrow ... sighing ... strength [failing].* At this stage Jesus feels sorrow at the realization that his vision has largely been rejected, and he feels drained by the tension and pressure of recent weeks.

The psalmist feels himself to be *a reproach to [his] enemies.* For Jesus, too, there have been many verbal duels both private and public, many sarcastic remarks, many challenges, many contemptuous dismissals. The psalmist feels himself to be a *dismay to those of [his] acquaintance. When they see [him] in the street they avoid [him].* This may well have been Jesus' experience as the situation became more dangerous and threatening. Fair-weather followers would by now be disappearing quietly from his company.

I have heard the whispering of the crowd; fear is all around; they put their heads together against me; they plot to take my life. These are the very reasons why Jesus made secret arrangements for the hiring of a beast for his procession.

But in the lovely closing verses, serenity is recovered as the future is handed over to God. *I have trusted in you, O Lord ... My times are in your hand.* In a few days Jesus will say something very like this in the Garden of Gethsemane.

Second Reading

Once again we are inside our Lord's head. I say this reverently because I do not wish to say that we can somehow analyze how or what our Lord thought. Yet the writer is trying to give us some idea of Jesus' attitude to his own identity and his work.

Jesus *did not regard equality with God as something to be exploited.* I find myself going back to Jesus' experience in the wilderness when he wrestled with the temptation to do exactly what Paul mentions here — to exploit his identity and his powers. Paul reminds us now that Jesus was determined not to do this.

There is an insight here for all of us. We are certainly not equal with God, but each of us has been given an identity and the gifts that go with it. As our Lord did not use his abilities exploitively — that is, for his own advantage — so we are called not to use our gifts for our own advantage alone. We are called to exercise them also in the service of others.

Jesus *emptied himself ... humbled himself and became obedient to the point of death.* While this degree of self-sacrifice is not asked of all of us — though it is certainly true that one day we will have to become obedient to death — each of us is asked to do some self-emptying. We can recall the expression, "He is full of himself," and we all know what it means. Our Lord calls us to the very opposite — to empty ourselves of the self whose demands can become insatiable, so that we have room for other selves.

Paul points out that such self-emptying and self-humbling is nothing less than the road to our Lord's glory. From it emerges his greatness. When we bow before this greatness we are by a glorious paradox bowing to our Lord's self-emptying.

Some echo of this truth applies in our own lives. We discover that the degree to which we can empty the self of its longing for attention and possession and status is the degree to which our spirituality gains authenticity and draws others to it and becomes grace for them.

The Gospel

This is the story that lies at the heart of the Christian faith. We have not heard it all. The rest of the story will bring a time of song and music and joy, because we will celebrate the fact that the death we have witnessed is not the end of the story. Yet we need to guard against lessening the death and hurrying to the resurrection.

The terror of the story is that God became like us so that we might become like God. Instead we became like demons. We hated, we betrayed, we condemned, we rejected, we killed. But this person whom we betrayed, condemned, and killed never condemned in return, never retaliated, never even defended himself. When we came to the point of actually killing him, he offered us forgiveness.

In this story of a killing, everyone involved reacts in some way to the prisoner. But he himself seems to stand alone, saying and doing very little. There is about him an awe-inspiring serenity. There is no word of pleading, protesting, or justifying himself. Some people desert him, some attack him, some question him, some strike him, some sneer. One person officially condemns him. Finally he is killed in the name of a great empire.

As we watch and listen to all this, it is hard not to feel that somehow Jesus is the one in charge. It is as if all the people around him are playing out their part in a great play in which they never meant to get involved, but here they are and they must act out their part. Perhaps this is another way of saying what Christian faith has always maintained. Jesus sacrificed himself, believing that if he, having assumed the human nature we all share, gave back this same human nature to God absolutely freely and willingly, he would give all men and women a glimpse of what their own human nature could rise to.

Down through the centuries this mystery has been expressed in many ways. Sometimes we have said that he became like us, so that we might become like him. At other times we have used the image of our Lord descending to the human, so that he might lift the human to God. Whenever we celebrate eucharist, we use another image: *Lamb of God, you take away the sin of the world: have mercy on us.*

Remember that all the people in this story are reacting in different ways to the prisoner. The High Priest reacts with anger, Pilate with curiosity, the soldiers with contempt, some in the crowd with hatred, the centurion in charge of the squad with admiration.

Now comes an important question about the reaction of one more person who is present in all this — you. What is your reaction to Jesus of Nazareth? All those people in the story lived their lives and made their decisions long ago. You are alive today, full of possibilities for God. What is your reaction? What is your decision?

Easter Day

Acts 10:34–43
Psalm 118:1–2, 14–24
1 Corinthians 15:1–11
John 20:1–18

Weavings

*Our fascination with printed text sometimes makes us forget
that in passages like these we are encountering other persons.
We are hearing their excited voices — let's not forget this excitement — as two men and a woman witness to us and to
others about the shattering event they have become involved
in, the resurrection of our Lord.*

*When we have read the scripture, we might think of these
three people turning to us, looking out from the text at us, and
asking for our response.*

Reflections

First Reading

On Easter Day, when we meet for the act of worship that is
central to our life as Christians, we are not immediately taken

to the tomb where our Lord rises. This happens in the gospel reading.

The very first thing we encounter is a crowd of people assembled in the house of a Roman centurion. Peter has come here by Cornelius's invitation. Both men have been shaken to the core by a dream. When they meet, they realize that their dream has drawn them together, and that their meeting has brought about the shattering of all Peter's lifelong Jewish assumptions. Unbelievable though it may appear, the Spirit of God is now reaching out to all humanity. This is the moment when we hear Peter addressing the assembled company.

I truly understand that God shows no partiality, but in every nation anyone who fears him and does what is right is acceptable to him. I suspect that, if we could have been present to hear Peter say these words, we would have caught a certain tentativeness in his voice, as if he could not yet fully believe what he heard himself saying. I am fairly sure that there were tears in his eyes and a tremor in his voice. Why not? It is one of the great turning points in his life and in the life of the gospel.

Peter now speaks of his own people. *You know the message [God] sent to the people of Israel, preaching peace by Jesus Christ.* Then he immediately reiterates his newly discovered understanding that Jesus Christ *is Lord of all.* Peter wants to stress that anything he now says about this Jesus applies to anyone who wishes to respond to him.

The rest of what Peter has to say is a kind of early credal statement.

John announced a baptism.
God anointed Jesus of Nazareth with the Holy Spirit.
He went about doing good and healing ...
God was with him.

We are witnesses to all that he did ...
They put him to death by hanging him on a tree ...
God raised him on the third day
To appear ... to us who were chosen by God as witnesses.
We ate and drank with him after he rose from the dead.
He commanded us to preach ... that he is the one ordained
by God as judge of the living and the dead.

It is important for every one of us to be able to make a coherent statement of our understanding of our Christian faith. What we say or write might be very different from this statement from Peter, but the important point is to possess a statement of faith that makes sense to ourselves. It is so easy for us to think of such statements of faith as emanating from great figures of the faith like Peter, or from the church as an institution, or from some already existing document such as our prayer book. All these are to be used and valued. But there must also be a statement of faith that is truly our own. It may reflect the "official" ones, or it may differ from them in various ways, but at least we have something to place beside the faith of the whole community, to compare and to contrast.

Peter tells us why this is important. He says, *Jesus went about doing good and healing;* and then he says, *We are witnesses to all that he did.* It follows that we today are also called to be witnesses. How can we witness to our Lord in any way unless we have decided ourselves what we believe about him and have found some form, however simple and tentative, of expressing it?

Peter comes back to this same theme of being witnesses. He continues to tell the listening crowd in Cornelius's house what he believes about Jesus: *God raised him on the third day and allowed him to appear ... to us who were chosen by God as witnesses.* Once again, those who have identified themselves with Jesus Christ are called in some sense to witness. This may not necessarily mean preaching sermons, haranguing friends, distributing earnest pamphlets. It may mean a quiet and implicit witness by the quality of our lives and our worshipping life. But behind even a quiet and implicit witness there must be some understanding of what one is witnessing to.

This passage ends with a statement whose good news for ourselves we can easily miss. *Everyone who believes in him receives forgiveness of sins through his name.* To understand this statement at the heart of Christian faith is to be given a great gift of mental, psychological, and spiritual worth. If I believe that Jesus has transformed the human nature that I share with him, then my human nature is redeemed from its own brokenness and shortcomings. In spite of who and what I am, I am acceptable to a loving God. If this is true, then I become acceptable to myself. When this happens in our lives, dawn breaks, burdens are lifted, joy is possible, peace reigns.

The Psalm

The way in which this psalm serves the theme of this Easter Sunday is a good example of how the psalms, like all poetry, can speak on many levels.

First, the psalm can be read as the psalmist wrote it, presumably out of his own experience. He has come through an extremely testing time. From the sound of certain phrases like *I shall not die, but live,* and *the sound of exultation and victory in the tents of the righteous,* he may have survived an actual battle. The rest of the song is a celebration of his survival and his gratitude for the gift of life.

But a second way to read the psalm is to connect it with Easter. Our Lord Jesus Christ has gone through an experience of death and he *shall not die, but live ... The Lord has punished [him] sorely, but he did not hand [him] over to death.* Death was not able to keep him. We might say that death has been defeated and life has been victorious. The psalmist uses an image that reverberates down the ages: *The same stone which the builders rejected has become the chief cornerstone.* This image perfectly describes the irony of the one who is rejected by the powers and institutions of his time but has become the cornerstone of faith for millions.

A third way to read these lines is to understand that they express some of our own personal experiences. At times when we have been deeply threatened, we may have thought, if not actually said, *I shall not die, but [I shall] live,* and then we have felt the thrill of great fear passing. At such times we, too, have felt the urge to give thanks. We have felt the surge of new life and new energy and new purpose. In this sense we have risen. We want to call out, *On this day the Lord has acted; we will rejoice and be glad in it.*

Second Reading

The real power of this passage lies in three short sentences within it. They occur at different points, but together they are the heart of the matter.

> *I would remind you … of the good news that I proclaimed to you ….*
> *I handed on to you … what I in turn had received.*
> *Last of all … he appeared also to me.*

Notice how deeply personal these three statements are. Paul is excited about what he has told his people, not only because Christ is risen and has appeared, but because this risen Christ has appeared to him — to Paul himself. This personal witness is what makes Paul's message powerful. That Christ has appeared to many others is merely information, however startling. But to Paul it has become much more than information because he himself has known the presence of the risen Christ. Information has been replaced by personal experience. He is a witness.

For us also, the way to authentic faith is to seek in our own experience the moments when for us Christ rose, when for us the presence of Christ became known — even if this knowing was fleeting and imperfectly understood. To follow the example of Paul in this passage is to give authenticity to our own efforts to be faithful witnesses.

We may find it difficult to describe any moment in our lives as being one in which we encountered the risen Lord, but it is certainly there, hidden, unrecognized, waiting to be discovered for what it truly was. We may feel that to claim an experience of Christ's resurrection in our own lives is to claim too much for ourselves. Who am I to make such a claim for some personal moment in my life? My excruciatingly ordinary faith journey does not merit my making claims of encounters with the risen Christ. In this sense, to use Paul's phrase, *I am the least ...*

Paul, like us, is only too aware of the extreme unlikelihood of Jesus ever encountering him, but he then spells out a great truth. There may be many reasons why my life is utterly unworthy of the gift of an encounter with my Lord, but *by the grace of God I am what I am, and his grace toward me has not been in vain.* So let me recognize a moment of that grace, for it is surely true that any such moment of grace involved the presence for me of the risen Lord. When we take hold of this great truth within ourselves, we become authentic witnesses. As Paul puts it, *so we proclaim and so you have come to believe.*

The Gospel

(This passage is the Easter gospel in all three years of the lectionary; so you may wish to look also at the reflections for this Sunday in Years A and C. Meanwhile here are some suggestions for a third way of interpreting the passage.)

Let us think of Mary as anyone today who is undertaking a spiritual search — a search for meaning and direction in life.

Early on the first day of the week ... Mary came to the tomb while it was still dark. We know immediately that her coming is full of anxiety and intensity. Much of the contemporary spiritual search is anxious and intense.

Mary ... saw that the stone had been removed from the tomb ... she ran ... and said ... "They have taken the Lord out of the tomb." Mary was wrong. She saw something she did not expect to find and immediately concluded that Jesus' body had been taken. Anyone who is searching today might assume that the spiritual quest involves the church, and yet on looking at the life and worship of the church, might see things that are uninviting, unwelcoming, unattractive, incomprehensible. It would be easy to conclude that somehow the Lord we are seeking has been in some way taken from us. Like Mary, we would be wrong.

Mary ... ran and went to Simon Peter and the other disciple, the one whom Jesus loved and told them. Mary did what anyone who feels spiritually vulnerable should do — she sought companionship. Whether we turn to a friend whom we trust, or whether we find a small group in which we can feel comfortable, the important thing is to reach for companionship as we do our searching for faith.

Peter and the other disciple set out and went toward the tomb. And although she is not mentioned, Mary ran with them.

How else could she have been outside the tomb weeping when the disciples left it and returned to their homes? After we have found a group to travel with in our spiritual journey, the group journeys on together — like the group of Mary, Peter, and the other disciple whom Jesus loved. But notice that each of these three people has come to faith in the risen Lord one by one, by him or her self. Notice the sequence:

Simon Peter came ... and went into the tomb ...
Then the other disciple ... also went in ...
Mary stood weeping outside the tomb.

All three come to faith on this day, but each arrives in his or her own way. Peter looks at the scene piece by piece, assembling the evidence. The other disciple seems to be much more intuitive. He looks and then leaps to faith. We all do this in our own way with the gifts God has given to us.

The two men go, leaving Mary in the area of the tomb. Whether she insisted on this we cannot tell. She is searching for more. She needs an experience of the risen Lord to know that he is indeed risen. She needs a sense of his presence. The very beautiful gift that Mary gives to us is her failure to recognize the Lord. So frequently in Christian experience when we seek the presence of our Lord, he comes in disguise. This is his way, as it is the way of God.

Jesus asks Mary, *Whom are you looking for?* Our Lord asks all of us this question. If we prefer, we can say that our Lord wishes all of us to ask ourselves this question. It is only when Mary realizes that the risen Jesus is not the same Jesus she has known before, that she is able to say with great joy and deep peace, *I have seen the Lord.* In our own time, it is very often true that a person searching for meaningful Christian faith is seeking in the terms and images and language and concepts that he or she encountered years ago, often in childhood or youth. Now this faith looks different, and it is easy to come to the sad — and sometimes angry and resentful — conclusion that our Lord is no longer present.

Do not hold on to me, says our Lord to Mary — and to all of us. We cannot take hold of our Lord in the way in which we first encountered him, especially if this was in childhood. That way of holding him, and being held by him, was wonderfully right for the time. But now there will be another way to hold and be held.

Second Sunday of Easter

Acts 4:32–35
Psalm 133
1 John 1:1—2:2
John 20:19–31

Weavings

In all these readings we sense a strong presence of community.
*   In the first reading, we glimpse the almost ecstatic dawning of the Christian community in the days after the Pentecostal experience. In vivid images from liturgy and nature the psalmist praises the value of unity. In the second reading, John writes to a close community that draws its life from the life and light of Christ. In the gospel, we are with the very first community gathered fearfully as it experiences the presence of the risen Lord.*

Reflections

First Reading

Now the whole group of those who believed were of one heart and soul. One suspects that Luke wrote this sentence with more than a little wistfulness. By the time he was writing his book, those who believed were certainly not of one heart and soul. This idyllic state — if it were ever present — did not last very long. In chapter six of Luke's book (The Acts) we begin to hear the rumblings.

But in this reading we see an image of the ideal community and can make some educated guesses about how it may have worked. First, we know from Paul's later activities that the community in Jerusalem had a number of very needy people in it. Second, we know that Jewish society was strongly committed to responding to needs among its own. It would be natural for this commitment to be mirrored in the new community, which had arisen out of a Jewish context. Third, we might consider the pattern that already existed in another community not very far away — the Qumran community — where all property was no longer private but given to the community.

Even more important was the influence, clearly evident in this short passage, of the original apostolic circle. Quite obviously this small group is showing immense courage in their unapologetic and fearless public *testimony to the resurrection of the Lord Jesus.* That members of the community *laid (the proceeds) at the apostles' feet* would suggest that great authority has already been invested in the apostolic group.

In this passage we get our first glimpse of the Christian community. It is not yet even called Christian, but these people are our ancestors in the faith. They are the first fruits of our Lord's ministry. Not long before he died, he said that, when he was lifted up, he would draw all people to him. The men and women in this passage are the first of those people. Probably the very cross on which he had been crucified was at this time still standing on the execution ground west of the city. Even now, before the evidence of his death is removed, his risen power has brought into being a people that will spread across the world and continue through time. We who read this passage today are this very people in our own time.

The Psalm

Oh, how good and pleasant it is, when brethren live together in unity! The psalmist sounds an expression of immense longing. Unity is one thing we long for in today's society, and one thing we find impossible to achieve. The psalmist reaches for the most extravagant images to describe how intensely he longs for unity. To us the images may seem bizarre, but if we are ready to enter his world of reference they make sense.

It is like fine oil upon the head that runs down upon the beard. One can tell that the images are crystal clear for him, as if he were a child watching something utterly incomprehensible yet marvellously crazy and forbidden. He imagines the moment in the liturgies of his people when oil is poured on the priestly figure. Rich and smooth and gleaming, it plasters his hair, glistens on his face, runs down the furrows of his neck, and seeps into the material of his robe — and he doesn't care! He revels in it because it is the oil of God and he feels caressed by it, nourished by it, cleansed and energized! This, the psalmist suggests to us, is what unity feels like when people discover it.

But he is not finished. *It is like the dew of Hermon that falls upon the hills of Zion.* He lives in northern Galilee, perhaps upon what is today called the Golan, where the distant snow-capped peak of Mount Hermon provides the backdrop for people's lives.

It affects their seasons and their crops, and brings an early morning dew. Like the oil for the priest, this dew is the source of joy and hope and life. This, too, sings the poet, is what it can be like to live together in unity.

As we read these verses today, they call us to strive for unity, to taste its elusive and hard-won sweetness, to come to know the energy it can release among us and the blessings it can bring.

Second Reading

Some time has gone by, perhaps a whole generation, since the scene described in the first reading. By now very few people still living can recall seeing the Lord in person. There has always been a tradition in the church that the author of this letter may have been John, the youngest of the apostles. It is just possible that when he writes, *what we have heard, what we have seen with our eyes ... and touched with our hands,* he does in fact refer to himself. Yet it seems more likely that *we* refers to the community as a whole. The writer may be saying that, because some heard and saw and touched the Lord in their lifetime, therefore all Christians in any time can hear and see and touch him.

The passage hints that the writer is addressing a community not entirely at one about how Christian faith should affect behaviour. He uses the word *fellowship* a number of times, as if he feels the need to encourage it. The pivotal sentence seems to be, *If we say that we have fellowship with him while we are walking in darkness, we lie and do not do what is true.* In these words we are hearing the tension between belief and action that occurs frequently in the New Testament communities. Paul was extremely stern about this incongruency in his letters, especially to the community in Corinth, and James also wrote a letter that concentrates on this issue.

We can hear intimations of argument in the second half of the passage, where indignant voices seem to protest about the writer's insistence on the link between belief and behaviour: *but we do have fellowship with our Lord! We are not sinning! We are not walking in darkness!* As we all well know, the tension between belief and behaviour was never to be resolved in the Christian community. We have only to look around us and, if truth be told, within ourselves.

The Gospel

The event itself is described in a way that makes it vivid and immediate. The mention of *evening ... doors ...locked for fear* points us to a group of men and women who are in shock. Their dream ended, their leader butchered like an animal, their hope for the future shattered, they are huddled in hiding.

Without warning of any kind the very person they mourn is among them. There is no hint of denial about what has happened. The ghastly wounds are there to see: *he showed them his hands and his side.* Quite understandably, the group is transformed. *The disciples rejoiced when they saw the Lord.*

Jesus now does something we can all too easily take for granted. He offers them his peace. Then he says, *As the Father has sent me, so I send you.* How has the Father sent Jesus? Into the world of affairs, struggles, ambiguities, dangers, challenges. In other words, the sending of Jesus is the very opposite of what these men and women are doing in this locked room. Our Lord moved in freedom; they have made themselves prisoners of their own fears. Our Lord reached out to others; they are avoiding all contact with others.

I send you. Our Lord does not dismiss these men and women because of their fears or because of their inability to rally in the face of events. He still regards them as worthy instruments for his purposes and gives them his peace to strengthen them.

We see this often in scripture. God will call a man or woman who will seem utterly unworthy of the call or unable to respond to it. Yet God will still call them to the task set before them. To recognize this pattern in scripture is to find very good news for ourselves. We are not dismissed as unworthy for service merely because of our fears or our many shortcomings.

We now move to the incident involving Thomas. He is not in the room at this moment. We will never know why he was gone, but he returns to find everyone transformed. They cluster around him, each wanting to be the first with the unbelievable news. To their dismay, Thomas spurns their efforts.

This is in keeping with Thomas' personality. Thomas is the consummate realist. Look back to the argument about whether they should return to Bethany after the news of the death of Lazarus (John 11:7–16). At that time Thomas had no illusions about the danger. Here in the crowded room full of voices, Thomas cuts through the euphoria with the emphatic refusal to believe them. Every deliberate word conveys the tone of his voice: *Unless I see the mark of the nails in his hands, and put my finger in the mark of the nails and my hand in his side, I will not believe.* It sounds almost as if Thomas is being deliberately brutal in expressing his conditions for believing.

A week passes. This simple statement is tantalizing. What was said in those first days of the church's life, what moods swept them from time to time, what plans were discussed and argued about? All we know is that the Lord once again came among them. As before, the arrival is unexpected, unannounced. Notice how the writer tells us again that *the doors were shut.* Once again we are reminded of the early self-induced imprisonment of the community, the very state from which the risen Lord wishes to release them, calling them into action and involvement.

It is Thomas who is immediately addressed. Our Lord's directions are a direct response to Thomas's previously spelled-out conditions. We are not told whether Thomas did in fact reach out to touch Jesus. But we do know that he burst out with the exclamation, *My Lord and my God!*

I have always felt that we are witnessing here the response of a person who is very far from being a doubter. I see Thomas as the very opposite: a deeply committed believer whose belief has been wounded and broken by the events of previous days. I see him as the kind of person who, when he makes a commitment to someone or something, makes a total commitment. He had committed himself to Jesus a few years before, and has stayed with him through thick and thin. Now his heart is broken by the ghastly death of Jesus, his world is collapsed, and he is determined never to give his heart to anything again, never to trust life again, never to give his love again. But when our Lord stands in front of him, Thomas gives himself totally once more. Ironically nicknamed the doubter, he is actually the classic believer. He wants to believe, needs to believe, must believe. Is Thomas alone in this?

Third Sunday of Easter

Acts 3:12–19
Psalm 4
1 John 3:1–7
Luke 24:36b—48

Weavings

All through this season we are witnessing the formation of the early Christian community. In the first reading, we are with Peter as he uses an incident of healing to speak of his Lord. In the psalm, we hear an echo of Peter's accusatory tone in the psalmist's challenge to the people. In the second reading, we begin to learn the characteristics by which the new community will be identified. In the gospel, we are present with the community when it receives another visitation from the risen Jesus.

Reflections

First Reading

We have arrived on the scene after a man has been healed in the Temple area, the most public place the healing could have happened. Luke seems to hint that Peter and John have not really intended to make this a moment of public discussion. They are on their way to a time and place of prayer late in the afternoon, and are passing the lame man when he asks them for alms. Instead of offering money they offer healing, and the man is indeed healed. As soon as this happens he rushes around, celebrating his new-found ability to walk, shouting and gesticulating in his excitement. This draws a crowd that eventually confronts the apostles in the covered area once frequented by Jesus and known as Solomon's Portico. Only at this stage does Peter decide to use the opportunity to address the crowd. It is significant that it is Peter who speaks, rather than the younger and probably more timid John. There is always the risk of volatility in a crowd, and it seems at first surprising that Peter's response is so confrontational. Note the self-distancing implicit in his opening words: *You Israelites.*

Peter's purpose is immediately apparent. He wishes to make no claim for his own powers in this matter. The source of healing is none other than the person *whom you handed over and rejected.* His confrontational tone becomes marked with a certain bitterness when he points out that the rejection occurred even *though [Pilate] had decided to release him.*

Peter continues to escalate the confrontation: *you rejected ... you asked [for] a murderer ... you killed.* At the end of this attack on the crowd, he shouts for emphasis: *you killed the Author of life, whom God raised from the dead.*

Absolutely without fear Peter now points to John and to himself, declaring, *we are witnesses.* The statement and the circumstances make us think about our own faith and our own commitment to Christian faith and the church. In what sense are we prepared to say these simple but significant and self-revealing words, *we are witnesses?*

Peter now lays all credit for this healing at the feet of the risen Jesus. As he does so, his approach changes. Suddenly the accusing tone is gone. We hear the word *friends,* coupled with the forgiving statement, *I know that you acted in ignorance.* He adds, *as did also your rulers,* perhaps with an eye to future relationships between the new community and the authorities. But Peter has no sooner softened his tone than he hardens it again. His claim is now made clearly and explicitly. This Jesus is no less than the long-expected messiah. The people have rejected their messiah. Peter's charge is clear: *Repent therefore, and turn to God so that your sins may be wiped out.*

The Psalm

In our culture we tend to dialogue a great deal within ourselves — questioning, analyzing, sometimes agonizing. For the psalmist it is more natural to dialogue with God. When he cries out in distress and asks for his prayer to be heard, it is the voice of God we hear replying.

Here in this psalm God is obviously running out of patience with his people. *How long will you worship dumb idols and run after false gods?* Yet the reply is full of the unflinching faith of Judaism, in spite of God's rebuking tone: *the Lord does wonders for the faithful; when I call upon the Lord, he will hear me.* Even to this faith, God's response is sharp: *Tremble, then, and do not sin.*

The psalmist now tries a different approach. *Many are saying, "O that we might see better times!"* The plea expresses a very contemporary and understandable longing that echoes in every corner of our society.

We need to take note of the psalmist's change of tone from here on. Suddenly he offers a plea: *Lift up the light of your countenance upon us, O Lord.* It would seem that the very act of turning to God becomes itself a source of grace and hope and new life. Many people will attest to the truth of this experience in their own lives. *You have put gladness in my heart,* cries the psalmist, *more than when grain and wine and oil increase.*

There is a gladness of the heart that is not attached to prosperity. Beyond the struggles over our daily affairs, our ambitions, our successes, and our failures in personal and professional life, we can find mysterious grace in our relationship with God. Here we can sometimes find peace: *I will lie down in peace; at once I fall asleep; for only you, Lord, make me dwell in safety.*

Second Reading

Raymond Brown, the highly respected scholar, has suggested that John's letters are written to "the community of the beloved disciple," a particular community of Christians of deep devotion and rigorous discipline.

The writer begins with the uncompromising reminder that the mark of a true Christian community is the quality of love among its members. To our ears this statement seems obvious, yet we know all too well that it constantly brings us face to face with the deep divisions and alienations of contemporary congregational life, not to mention an individualism that judges everything by asking, "what does it give me?" or "what do I get out of this?"

Beloved, we are God's children now; what we will be has not yet been revealed. Notice that the writer looks at Christian believing not as a state but as a process, a growing and a maturing in the faith and in our relationship with our Lord. *What we do know is this: when he is revealed, we will be like him.* John is saying that to grow in Christian believing is to grow into the likeness of our Lord. To achieve this in any way and to any degree demands discipline in life, in thought, and in action. *All who have this hope in him purify themselves.*

To read this passage is to be made both thoughtful and modest in our spiritual self-assessing. Listen to the standard put before us: *No one who abides in him sins; no one who sins has either seen him or known him.* Such a statement is a long way from the casual standards most of us bring to our living out of Christian faith.

The Gospel

Jesus stood among them. The risen Lord is among his followers without warning. We need to remind ourselves that our Lord does indeed come among us. In a culture from which the transcendent has been diminished, if not crushed, it is not necessarily obvious that he does. We are apt to respond to statements such as this by asking if it is a theological, psychological, or sacramental truth. We want to analyze and define rather than bow our heads before a mystery.

Luke seems to imply by their reaction that the little group to whom the risen lord appeared is still very fearful and nervous. Or could this be the first appearance of our Lord to them since *they were startled and terrified, and thought they were seeing a ghost?*

For most contemporary Christians, Jesus is a kind of ghost — a historical memory or a figure in a tradition who is respected, prayed to, rendered in art or language, but essentially unreal.

A ghost does not have flesh and bones as you see that I have. We need to be wary of much contemporary Christian spirituality that is unwilling to acknowledge the validity and necessity of the church. We live in a time when spirituality is suspicious of structure and form and institution. Yet any spirituality, if it is to last through the vicissitudes of time and history, must take on form. It cannot remain a kind of ghost, but must assume a structure like *flesh and bones.*

They gave him a piece of broiled fish, and he took it and ate it in their presence. I hear this scripture telling me that sacrament will always be an essential part of the structure of Christian spirituality. Ordinary acts and ordinary things take on a significance far greater than themselves and convey the divine presence to us.

Then he opened their minds to understand the scriptures. Another element that will be fundamental in the future Christian community is holy scripture, an essential resource in our present struggle.

You are witnesses of these things. Every Christian has a task or ministry to carry out, however modestly and quietly they choose to do it. Each of us is called to communicate to others that the faith we hold gives meaning to life and grace for living. The belief that Christian faith is a merely a private matter runs in the face of scripture. It is an illusion that arises from the radical individualizing of Western culture, an individualizing that is already exacting a high cost in loneliness and in the fragility of relationships.

Fourth Sunday of Easter

Acts 4:5–12
Psalm 23
1 John 3:16–24
John 10:11–18

Weavings

As we read these passages, we hear again and again of one who has laid down his life for others. In the first reading, Peter proclaims this truth about Jesus to those who would prosecute him. The psalm assures us that in dying we have a companion who walks the valley of death with us. In the second reading, John begins with the categorical statement of our Lord's sacrifice, and draws consequences for our behaviour. In the gospel passage, Jesus emphasizes the distinguishing mark of the good shepherd — his readiness to sacrifice himself for the flock.

Reflections

First Reading

The authorities have become aware that something is among them that cannot be ignored. A measure of their alarm is that *rulers, elders, and scribes assembled in Jerusalem, with Annas the high priest, Caiaphas, John, and Alexander, and all who were of the high-priestly family.* A closely knit establishment with many vested interests has decided to close ranks quickly and solidly against the danger.

For us there is more significance in this confrontation between the new Christian faith and the Jewish authorities than a historical recollection. There are at least two places in today's world where hearers of this passage would identify with it immediately. Those two places — and there are certainly more — are Indonesia and the Sudan. In each of these countries Christians are experiencing a concerted effort to destroy them and their faith. In each of these countries the power structure acting against Christians is a closely woven network of family power allied with those who owe their power to the ruling family or tribe. The reason given for attacks on Christians is never religion. Instead, Christians are accused of disloyalty and subversion. Christians wish to disturb the peace. They are allied to enemies of the state. They wish to form a separate political entity independent of the state. For all these reasons it becomes permissable — even essential — to attack them.

By what power or by what name did you do this [healing]? Peter has left not the slightest doubt that this healing was done not by him but through him. This says something very important to us as the ministry of healing begins again to take its rightful place in the life of the church. To offer oneself in congregational life for this ministry does not depend on some mysterious or powerful capacity to heal people. One offers oneself not as a source of healing but as a channel of Christ's healing. One's gifts for a ministry of healing depend on one's capacity to get out of the way of our Lord's healing, letting it take place through us. When we lay hands on another, there need be no straining effort to feel something or to produce something. We are most useful to this ministry when we can let go and offer our whole being as an instrument for our Lord's work. Listen to Peter's way of saying it: *this man is standing before you in good health by the name of Jesus Christ of Nazareth.*

As we argue and discuss the role of the church in today's world, it is salutary to recall that the issue in these earliest confrontations between church and society was healing. The primary vocation felt by the men and women of those first Christian days was a call to heal. Is this saying something to us about contemporary Christian vocation? *Jesus Christ of Nazareth, whom you crucified ... God raised from the dead.* We are told here that the power to heal follows death and resurrection. Is it possible that the return of the ministry of healing to the life of so many congregations is itself a sign of resurrection in the church as the body of Christ?

This Jesus ... has become the cornerstone. There is salvation in no one else, for there is no other name under heaven given among mortals by which we must be saved. Many hear this statement of Peter as the basis for the dismissal of all faiths other than Christian. But we need to hear it in context. Peter is utterly alive with the sense of the Lord's being risen and alive. For Peter there cannot be any origin other than our Lord for what he feels within himself. He has no need of any other source of grace. But isn't this also true for any Christian who has become newly aware of the presence of our Lord in his or her life? When a person comes alive with Christ, there is a sense of utter completion, and no other source of grace is needed or sought. So it is with any true religious conversion in any of the great faiths. When faith is ignited in one's own heart and mind, that faith is all-sufficing.

The Psalm

If we consider the psalm as in some way an echo of the reading we have just heard, then we might ask how the portrait of the early Christian community in Jerusalem becomes, in turn, an echo of this psalm.

We see a portrait of a group of people who are utterly sure of where their allegiance lies. For them, Jesus is the source of meaning, the reference point for every aspect of their lives. Their courage, their energy, their determination all emerge from this extraordinary trust in him as Lord. The psalm asks for this same degree of trust. It begins by assuming an attitude of complete dependence upon God: *The Lord is my shepherd, I shall not be in want.*

He makes me lie down in green pastures and leads me beside still waters. The very first thing that God encourages us to do is the very last thing our culture wants us to do — be still. God wishes me to be still because stillness is the very quality that *revives my soul.* The gift of stillness is followed by God's second gift — a sense of direction. He *guides me along right pathways.* These pathways will not always be sun-filled and care-free. Sometimes I will be led through shadows and even deep darkness. God does not give guarantees that my path will always avoid such places, but God does promise that I will not walk alone. *You [God] are with me.* This is the single thing of which I can be sure.

If it is true that God will walk with me even in the dark places, it follows that in those same places I will find a source of grace. I will always receive nourishment for my spirit. There will always be a *table*, food for my soul; *oil*, balm for my soul; a *cup*, drink for my soul.

The final lines become a celebration of what I have learned to be true of God. Once again there is the promise of companionship for my journey. *Goodness and mercy shall follow me* — another way of saying that I will have the company of God. In these last lines are expressed two modes of life — travelling on a journey, and being at home. On my journey I will know that God's mercy and goodness follow me. And also on my journey I will have a sense of being always at home in God's presence. *I will dwell in the house of the Lord for ever.*

Second Reading

If there is a place in the new testament where we have a charter of Christian behaviour, this is it:

> *We know love by this,*
> *that he laid down his life for us —*
> *and we ought to lay down our lives for one another.*

This sentence has a devastating simplicity and an awe-inspiring directness, both in what it says about our Lord and in what it demands of those of us who call him Lord.

John proceeds to spell it out in equally simple but equally challenging specifics. To lay down one's life for another does not always call for the ultimate sacrifice made by our Lord. It can emerge from our overall attitude to others. It can come about in the simplest of human responses to another's need. Christian faith is inseparable from the use we make of *the world's goods*. In Christian faith, love is not just a heart-warming concept; it exists only *in truth and action*. Love in action is the single measure of the integrity of our professed faith. As John says, *by this we will know that we are from the truth.*

John now cuts through whatever complexities and elaborations we weave around Christian faith. The heart of faith is obedience to two commands that are utterly simple in expression but so profound that even a human life of the greatest sanctity is not sufficient to plumb their full meaning. *This is his commandment, that we should believe in the name of his Son Jesus Christ and love one another.*

In fact, the two elements of this commandment are one. To believe and to love is a single reality. Each gives strength to the other. When believing and loving are woven together in a human life, then we know that God abides in that life. We find ourselves reminded of the Taizé chant that sings, "Ubi caritas et amor, Deus ibi est": Where there is caring and love, there is God.

The Gospel

On one level this passage is simple and clear. We are listening to our Lord speaking to his disciples. He offers an image of himself that is utterly familiar to everyone in this society — the *good shepherd.* The term would have had as much significance for those listening as would *the good Samaritan.* Both shepherds and Samaritans were outsiders to the culture. Both were regarded as anything but good, deserving of contempt if not loathing. The shepherd did a tough, dirty, dangerous job that few wished to do. He was often a rough, tough individual with few illusions about how he was regarded, and therefore with few reasons to be either gracious or trustworthy. When our Lord speaks of himself as *the good shepherd,* he is fully aware of the role and image of a shepherd. He, too, sees himself as outsider, as in some sense rejected.

Jesus use the image for a reason. Shepherds were known to die protecting their flock. Already the shadow of the cross is falling over Jesus, yet the bond between him and those who have followed him is indissoluble. He will even die for them.

This passage is rich with many levels of meaning. It can speak to all human relationships. *The good shepherd lays down his life for the sheep.* The test is how much we will give for the relationship, whatever the cost to ourselves. Jesus speaks of the very different behaviour of a *hired hand.* To what extent are we in the relationship as a kind of hired hand — for what it pays us or for what we can get out of it?

Jesus says, *I have other sheep that do not belong to this fold. I must bring them also.* If this passage speaks to us about relationships, we may hear our Lord saying that it is not sufficient for us to invest all that we are in a single relationship. Every relationship calls for some cost of self-investment. All relationships call us to give rather than merely to take. Sometimes we feel that this is too draining, yet mysteriously, when we give ourselves to a relationship, we often find that we are actually energized.

Jesus says, *I lay down my life in order to take it up again.* He is referring to his resurrection, but the words are true for us on another level. How many times have we given ourselves to others to the point of weariness and even resentment — perhaps for a spouse in a difficult stage of marriage, or for a child in a difficult stage of development — only to encounter moments of response that energize and revitalize us. Having laid down our life, we take it up again.

Fifth Sunday of Easter

Acts 8:26–40
Psalm 22:24–30
1 John 4:7–21
John 15:1–8

Weavings

The theme I hear in all of these passages is the way God acts upon us and within us to form us spiritually.

In the first reading, something draws the African traveller on his journey towards the encounter that changes his life. This something is the Spirit of God acting on and in his human spirit. In the psalm, we hear the psalmist emerge from a sense of God's absence to a sense of God's grace-giving presence. In the second reading, we are told that our vocation as Christians is to embody the love of God as it was embodied in our Lord. In the gospel, our Lord himself tells us that a relationship with God in which God continues to form us is the source of our ability to live creatively and gracefully in the world.

Reflections

First Reading

Now there was an Ethiopian eunuch ... returning home; seated in his chariot. I can see this man travelling in his chariot, head down as he tries to read in a shuddering rocking vehicle, leaving behind the city he has just visited, facing a long and probably dangerous journey home.

He has most likely spent a great deal of money for the scroll he has purchased. Assuming that he could not take a great many things home, and that he did not have access to endless money and therefore had to make choices, it says a lot about him that this was his choice — a copy of the book we know as Isaiah. It says much about his taste because, as we know, he had selected to take with him the greatest voice and the loveliest language of all scripture.

We know, too, that he probably had a brilliant mind and could be trusted. The text tells us that he was not only a court official of his queen but also that he was *in charge of her entire treasury.*

I want to know why he came to Jerusalem in the first place. The text says that *he had come ... to worship.* Does this mean that he was a Jew? If so, how had he ended up in such a distant part of the world? His existence is an indication of how widespread the diaspora already was. I find myself trying to imagine his feelings as the towers and walls of Jerusalem disappeared behind him while he drove down towards the coast road to Gaza. Scripture tells us that this was the road he took. We can assume it was dangerous by Luke's quick aside: *This is a wilderness road.*

What was he seeking? Was he at a stage in life where he longed to return, even briefly, to his roots? Was he ill, knowing perhaps that he had not long to live, and therefore needed to make this journey to his spiritual home before returning to his earthly home to die? Was this why he bought the scroll? Did he need something tangible to help in the lonely and difficult time ahead?

It is obvious from the moment that Philip encounters him that this man is ripe for deep changes in his life. In more than one sense he is on a journey; and as his body journeys, so does his spirit. He longs for something he cannot yet define. Reading the scroll speaks to this longing. Why does this particular passage of Isaiah move him? Does he identify with the unknown figure who has experienced humiliation and suffering? Does he recognize experiences similar to his own?

All these things must remain questions. But we know that he responds with joy and eagerness to Philip's identifying of the scroll with the life of Jesus. For some reason it makes immediate and shattering sense. He has found what he has been looking for. In the deepest sense he has come home. We see Philip and him on a stretch of the road that may have turned towards the sea for a few miles. The two of them leave the chariot and go across the sands to the blue water. There, standing in the warm sea, the traveller and seeker allows himself to die for a moment in the supporting arms of Philip. Drawing deep gulps of air, he rises from the water and splashes his way back to the beach. There are a thousand things he wants to talk about, but Philip cannot stay. Yet in spite of his unanswered questions, the new follower of Jesus *went on his way rejoicing.*

There is something of all of us in this traveller. Like him, I am on a journey that is both outer and inner, physical and spiritual. Like him, much of my travelling takes place in a world and a culture that is a wilderness of the mind and the spirit. Like him, I am seeking without fully being able to describe or define what I seek. Like him, I go to various cities and have various experiences but must always leave again. Home is else-where than in the cities I visit. But even as I go home, I still seek the meaning of all the journeying within and without. What do I seek? Whom do I seek?

As the voice of Isaiah speaks to the traveller from his newly acquired and precious scroll, so I have the luxury of many more voices that speak to me in books, film, video, conferences, tapes, art, music. Like him, I have had — and still have — God-given companions on my journeying.

Finally, like this traveller from Ethiopia, I have often been given the precious gift of a Philip — more than one Philip — in growing years and through adult years — those many voices who have spoken to me of One who was born, lived, suffered, died, and rose. Like this traveller, I have felt the waters of bap-tism, albeit as a child. And like this traveller out of Africa, be-cause of the gift of Jesus of Nazareth given to me by these count-less Philips — friends and family in the community of faith — I am enabled, in spite of my humanity, to go on my way rejoicing.

Psalm

Just as we feel the resolution in the life of the man travelling home to Africa, so there is a great feeling of resolution in these verses. The whole psalm to this point has expressed distress. The psalmist has felt loneliness in his distress. He has felt God-forsaken. He has felt rejected by others, exhausted, beset by many enemies. The Ethiopian traveller would recognize these feel-ings. In the ancient world, the brilliant powerful eunuch, near as he was to the ear and mind of the ruler, developed enemies and was often lonely and vulnerable, knowing that he was both feared and hated.

Having expressed his personal agonies and burdens, the psalmist now breaks through to confidence. The presence of

God becomes real again and he can draw upon this presence as a source of strength. Once again he feels he can emerge and join others in worship. *My praise is of [God] in the great assembly ... kingship belongs to the Lord ... My soul shall live for him.*

Second Reading

This passage seems to be saying very simple and obvious things. After all, everyone knows that God is love, that we are to love, and so on. But this passage is important because here we are seeing the foundations of Christian life being laid down in the dawn of the new faith. We are listening to the voice of a great Christian mind thinking through what the encounter with Jesus has meant and will mean for all time for those who decide to follow him.

There is another reason that this passage is important. We may have heard the call to Christian love a million times, but the truth is that a great gulf yawns between knowing this and living it out day by day. Familiar though these lines may be, they need to sound in our ears again and again: *Beloved, let us love one another, because love is from God; every one who loves is born of God and knows God.*

Bring to mind for a moment the deep divisions at every level of Christian life today — the tensions within congregations, the deep distrust between different seminaries with different theologies of ministry, the resentments engendered between individuals and groups who have differently experienced the presence of our Lord. Given all this, we realize how necessary this passage is to our corporate life as Christians.

Perhaps most important of all is the writer's insistence that God takes the initiative in showing love towards us, who are very far from having earned or deserved it. *In this is love, not that we loved God but that he loved us.* Moreover, *if we love one another, God lives in us, and his love is perfected in us.* What an unimaginable affirmation of human nature — it is deemed worthy to be a vehicle for perfecting the love of God!

How can this be? Not because human nature lives in me, but because it has been embodied and transformed in Jesus Christ. *God abides in those who confess that Jesus is the Son of God, and they abide in God ... Love has been perfected among us in this.*

Towards the end of the passage, John returns to the blunt and direct style of the opening lines. *Whoever does not love does not know God.* John may be writing with some experience of community life in mind. But the statement brings us up short. *Those who say, "I love God," and hate their brothers or sisters, are liars.* We have only to read or hear this to know how deeply it addresses the fractured and contentious life of today's church.

The Gospel

We are listening to our Lord as his voice is recalled by John years after that night in the upper room.

I am the true vine, and my Father is the vinegrower. Here is another image by which we can think through our relationship with our Lord and with God. In stating his own relationship with God, Jesus is describing my relationship to God. The difference is that I am not a true vine. Only Jesus is the true vine. I am a very pathetic growth compared with my Lord.

In reading this passage I am struck by the fact that Jesus is speaking of himself when he says, *[God the vinegrower] removes every branch in me that bears no fruit.* If this is true of Jesus, how incalculably more is it true of me.

Another truth I see here is that, even when I do bear some fruit, the process of God's refining my whole being still goes on. *Every branch that bears fruit he prunes to make it bear more fruit.* Christian faith affirms my humanity in spite of its shortcomings. You and I are being asked to believe that God, the creator of infinities beyond our imagination, is actually at work in the microcosm of our individual souls.

Next come statements that challenge the radical individualism of our time. *The branch cannot bear fruit by itself unless it abides in the vine.* I am not created to live to myself or by means of myself. I am incomplete without the grace of others and without the grace of God who comes to me in Jesus Christ. To try to live to myself ensures that I *wither* away spiritually. Without the bond between God and my humanity, this humanity loses the capacity to be creative.

If you abide in me, and my words abide in you, ask for whatever you wish, and it will be done for you. Obviously we are not to take this statement of our Lord as giving us a blank cheque for all that we desire. I may very well do my human best to abide in Christ. I may do my human best to live a life that reflects his words. But I must still accept the limits and the costs of my fallen humanity. To the degree that I strive to abide in the Lord and to embody his words, to this same degree will I receive his grace to glorify him in my living, in spite of the flaws and brokenness of my life.

Sixth Sunday of Easter

Acts 10:44–48
Psalm 98
1 John 5:1–6
John 15:9–17

Weavings

In all of today's readings we are made conscious of a grace and a presence beyond ourselves, a reality we cannot control or direct.

In the first reading, we see the way the Spirit of God changes the lives of everyone present, shattering their assumptions and their limited thinking. The psalm praises the activity of God in human affairs, acknowledging God as judge of all. In the second reading, John reminds us that faith itself is not an achievement on our part but a gift from God. In the gospel, our Lord tells us that his power will give our human loves the power to do what he commands.

Reflections

First Reading

We are in a large room in the residence of a Roman army officer stationed in the coast city of Caesarea. Present are Cornelius himself and his family, a group of Jewish followers of Jesus who have come with the apostle Peter, and Peter himself. He is probably standing apart from the two groups because we know that he has been addressing them. The two men, Cornelius and Peter, have just been telling the group of the extraordinary way in which they have been brought together. Each has had a dream linking him to the other and bringing about this encounter. Peter has just made a statement so far from removed from everything he has hitherto believed that he can hardly believe he is actually saying it.

Up to now the new Jesus movement has kept within the bounds of Judaism. The movement is understood as merely a new form of Judaism. All the ancient Jewish customs are still being observed. Gentiles are still regarded as utterly outside even this new covenant made in Jesus. But Peter's vivid dream and his subsequent encounter with Cornelius is about to change everything. We listen as Peter speaks. He has told his dream to the group, and he has heard Cornelius tell his dream. Both can see that they have been drawn together by a power beyond themselves. Now in his opening words Peter expresses the vast leap he is about to make: *I truly understand that God shows no partiality.*

This is the moment when today's reading begins. The group listening to Peter realizes that something is happening to Cornelius and his family. The experience spreads to the Jewish believers. All have a distinct and shattering experience of the Holy Spirit within them. They begin to speak in tongues. When the experience passes, everyone in the room has changed forever. Peter and his Jewish companions can hardly believe what they have seen. Gentiles have been touched by God just as Jews have been.

There probably is a stunned silence after the intensity and fervour of the spiritual experience. Into this silence Peter calls out, *Can anyone withhold the water for baptizing these people who have received the Holy Spirit just as we have?* These last four short words are extremely important. As he spoke them, a certain awe must have crept into Peter's voice.

The joyful baptism of Cornelius and his family follows. When it ends, the new church has been changed. There is still much argument to come, even much painful confrontation, but there is no going back. Christian faith has broken out of the cocoon of Judaism in which it had been born. The doors have swung open.

Is there any sense in which we today are experiencing a great change of this kind? Has Christian faith to discover within itself a greater inclusiveness than it has hitherto known? Will it bring into being a language and images and symbols that can present Jesus Christ as an image of the universal God that calls to all men and women without diminishing the significance of the traditions which they already hold?

The Psalm

It feels like walking in on a huge party. The singing is deafening, the dancers are whirling, arms are waving, food and drink are everywhere. The house of Cornelius must have been full of the atmosphere of this psalm. Voices cry out: The Lord *has done marvellous things. The Lord has made known his victory.*

These people make no claim to having achieved victory. Everything is ascribed to God. *With his right hand and his holy arm has [God] won for himself the victory.*

The extraordinary thing about these people and their relationship with God is that, if they had just experienced defeat, they would still have approached this same God. This God remains God no matter what happens. All events are within the providence of this God — defeat or victory, bad times or good times, rich harvest or lean harvest. All is of God, and all aspects of life find their reason and their meaning in God.

It is this sublime faith that makes this party possible — the conviction that there is ultimate meaning in God and that, therefore, there is always hope for the future. *With trumpets and the sound of the horn shout with joy before the King.*

Human events are linked with the rest of creation as if the whole thing forms a vast symphony. *Let the sea make a noise ... Let the rivers clap their hands ... let the hills ring out with joy.*

We moderns with our tentative and fragmented beliefs stand at the edge of this party, envious of such a sure inner vision. The psalmist and his people offer it to us. Shall we accept it?

Second Reading

To believe in Jesus Christ is a gift of God. In a nutshell this is what John is telling us. He is also emphasizing that our love for God has to be rooted in our attitude to other people, especially those who share with us an allegiance to Jesus Christ. *By this we know that we love the children of God, when we love God and obey his commandments.* Once again we have to contrast this admonition from John with the reality we face in so much of contemporary church life, with its divisions among those who claim to share Jesus Christ as Lord but whose ways of comprehending and expressing that lordship differ widely.

In John's winsome statement that *whatever is born of God conquers the world,* we glimpse for a moment the bright light of the dawn of Christian faith. John is not writing about the pursuit of power by conquest. He is expressing a feeling similar to Wordsworth's reflecting on the French Revolution: "Bliss was it in that dawn to be alive, but to be young was very heaven!" The young heart of the church is beating fast; its eyes are wide with the wonder of new-found faith.

I say these things, not to insinuate that such excitement is no longer possible, but to remind us that Christian faith can still communicate such fervour. For many people today it still does. In a recent book entitled *Morning Light,* Jean Sullivan notes that many people find themselves weeping for the passing of the familiar forms of the church. But, she says, there is something much more important than weeping: "To create is the most important thing; to rediscover the fervour that formed the thing you are weeping for." I find that simple statement arresting.

Who is it that conquers the world but the one who believes that Jesus is the Son of God? Even outside and beyond Christian faith, those who have a belief system are in a far better position to struggle with life and the world than those who have none. To possess Christian faith as one's basis for meaning is to possess an immensely rich and deep resource for living in the world. Through this faith we can conquer life, not in the sense of dominating it, but in the sense of being conqueror rather than victim.

The Gospel

As in previous weeks we are sitting in the presence of our Lord, listening to him speaking quietly and intensely near the final hours of his earthly life. The intensity comes from his clear knowledge that he has little time left with these fragile and vulnerable people to whom he has entrusted his hopes for the future.

Of all the passages in John's gospel, this one is addressed most immediately to these disciples. One can easily imagine the scene. Our Lord probably seated, the others facing him from their various positions around the table. As he speaks, he makes eye contact again and again. This message is for them, and they are never to forget these quiet words. We who are today's disciples also must never forget these things.

Abide in my love. On several recent Sundays we have been reminded that this is the absolutely primary command. Significantly, Jesus does not say that we are to abide in love but, rather, *in my love.* We ourselves, whose capacity for love is limited, are not the source of the deepest and strongest love. To love faithfully and strongly we have to be aware of the source of love beyond our own.

If you keep my commandments, you will abide in my love. Abiding in the love of Christ is not an exercise in manufactured fervency or well meant sentimentality. To abide in the love of Christ is obedience to the challenges of loving, obedience to the task of overcoming the very human temptation to love only oneself.

Turning to the task of loving others, Jesus delivers his great commandment: *This is my commandment, that you love one another as I have loved you.* It is significant that when this statement is quoted, the last five words are frequently omitted. Not without good reason, because to love as Jesus has loved is to love without limit. Quite understandably this dismays and terrifies our limited human capacity for self-sacrificing love.

To assist us, our Lord makes a tremendous offer: *I do not call you servants any longer ... but I have called you friends.* Yet it is not easy for us to accept the privilege. I have noticed that the term *servant* appears in countless hymns, but rarely in hymnody are we called the friends of Christ.

Nor is it easy for us to accept that *you did not choose me but I chose you.* We feel like the psalmist when he says that *such knowledge is too wonderful for me ... I cannot attain to it.*

Or we feel like Peter in the boat on the lake when he is overcome by a sense of being utterly unworthy of the friendship he has encountered in Jesus.

Finally, we are given simply and directly our vocation, our marching orders: *I appointed you to go and bear fruit, fruit that will last.* Can we measure up to this great demand? Of ourselves we cannot. But we are not alone. There is one further word for us: *the Father will give you whatever you ask in my name.*

Seventh Sunday of Easter

Acts 1:15–17, 21–26
Psalm 1
1 John 5:9–13
John 17:6–19

Weavings

These readings point to certain qualities in Christian faith like faithfulness, resilience, and intentionality.

In the first reading, we encounter a person who embodies these qualities to the extent that he is seen as a potential apostle in the circle of the twelve. The psalm celebrates those who are well planted and whose lives bear fruit for God. In the second reading, we are called to a faith that is deep and confident. In the gospel, we hear our Lord praying that the faith of those who follow him may respond to the testing of life in the world.

Reflections

First Reading

It is some weeks after the stunning experience of our Lord's resurrection. Weeks have elapsed since the small, newly-born community was hiding behind locked doors. They have emerged with a vengeance! Some of them have acted very publicly in the name of the risen Lord. Some have felt the wrath of the authorities but have stood up to it and so far survived. In past Sundays we have been witnesses to such events.

The event we are now about to witness is not public. It deals with important matters of the inner life of the community. A shadow has been cast over everyone by the memory of Judas's betrayal and his subsequent suicide. It has broken the circle of the twelve made by the Lord himself. Great significance was given to this number, which linked the apostles with the twelve tribes of their history as a people. Now the time has come to act to restore the circle.

Two men are proposed, and the simple method of election proceeds after a prayer is said. Matthias is elected. He is placed in the circle, and once again the community feels complete. The terrible wound of betrayal and tragic death is healed.

We know nothing about Matthias. No act of his has been reported, no word handed on. He is as unknown as Justus, who also stood for election. But there are a few things we can infer from the situation in which we meet them.

Notice the criteria for the election. Peter tells the community that they are looking for someone *who has accompanied us during all the time that the Lord Jesus went in and out among us, beginning from the baptism of John until the day when he was taken up from us.* Whoever is to be elected must have joined the community in its earliest days and remained faithful to it all through the thick and thin of what followed. This included many times of threat towards Jesus and his supporters, many times of actual danger, not to mention the agony and terror of the trial and subsequent ghastly death. Matthias must have shared the fear and the hopelessness, and then when the risen Lord came among them, his eyes must have blazed with joy and hope.

We can infer that Matthias had an immense capacity to remain faithful. The collect for Saint Matthias's day refers to those who are "faithful" and remain "steadfast," and in the gospel for his day we hear our Lord use the word *abide* no less than seven times. Matthias was the sort of person one could depend on to abide — to hang in and be faithful.

Matthias turns up often in the life of parish churches, especially in large churches, the kind we today call corporate parishes. These are the people you never really get to know beyond a shake of the hand or a fleetingly exchanged smile. At first they may volunteer a name, but it never settles in anyone's mind, and they remain anonymous in a quiet and faithful way. Months go by, even years, until something happens, or something is said, revealing that a great soul dwells within this person. Sometimes a whole congregation comes to realize that someone of great courage and faithfulness or generosity has been hidden within its life. I call these people our Matthiases.

The Psalm

The text of the psalm is a clear and immediate echo of the reading. Once again we are being shown two images of the land. We walk past *trees planted by streams of water,* and then suddenly we must bend forward and guard our eyes and faces from the sting of *chaff which the wind drives away.*

I often think that these utterly contrasting images are natural to a writer who lives in a very small country. In Israel, it is only a short distance from desert to oasis, or from bare brown hills to plains and valleys of waving grass or corn. One is constantly made aware of the varied tapestry of physical geography. Consequently, the varied tapestry of psychological geography — human character and experience — also comes to mind. Once again, the trees and the chaff stand for choices we all make in life. What course do we choose to follow? What companions do we choose for the journey? *Happy are they who have not walked in the counsel of the wicked.*

What is essential in life? Nowadays we are fond of using the term *centred.* We speak of looking for a centre. The psalm is responding to this search, but it says that we make a mistake if we think that we will find the centre in our own selves. This point is easy to miss, because of the language of the psalmist. When he says, *Happy are they [whose] ... delight is in the law of the Lord,* he is suggesting that the centre we seek lies beyond ourselves. This does not mean that we should not examine ourselves. It does not mean that we cannot plumb the depths of our souls, as we do our searching. But it is telling us that, at the end of all our striving and journeying, the discovery that the centre for the self lies within God will satisfy that same self more than anything else. Just as a tree takes its life from the water outside itself, so we are born to draw life from God. Just as the water enables such trees to bear *fruit in due season,* so our decision to draw energy and inspiration for our lives from God will enable us to live creatively and effectively in the world.

Second Reading

It comes as a shock to realize how differently we think than did the writer of this passage.

The whole tone of this scripture is one of either/or. Lines are drawn simply and starkly. There is no middle ground in the matter of Christian faith. *Whoever has the Son has life; who-*

ever does not have the Son of God does not have life. Try to calculate how many millions of miles this statement is from our passion to be inclusive, non-judgemental, and politically correct, and to show all the other virtues of our post modern world!

Let us go back a little in the passage. *This is the testimony: God gave us eternal life, and this life is in his Son.* Notice the precise and deliberate tone. For the writer, this is the heart of the matter. This, we should remind ourselves, is the heart of the matter for us too. It is the heart of the matter for Christians in any age.

Think of some time in your life when you held something with deep passion, utter acceptance, and the conviction that for you at that moment this was the most significant thing in the world. Discovering that you are in love with another person, and that he or she is in love with you, can be such a moment. I think this is a good image for describing the encounter with Jesus Christ that many people experience. I can attest to it from my own experience.

Out of this intensity of experience John writes. He and other Christians are utterly convinced that their relationship with Jesus Christ has given them a quality of being alive that puts them in touch with ultimate reality. They express this experience in the phrase *eternal life.* This quality of being alive is so deep, so all-embracing, that once they possess it, they cannot conceive of its being available from any other source.

Such feelings, and the instinctive exclusivism that goes with them, are perfectly understandable. Most of us learn later in life that, while our relationship with our Lord remains deep, while it provides us with a foundation for life and meaning that nurtures and guides — and judges — us, others find their sources of nurture and meaning in other ways. Yet their ways are no less of God than the revelation and the relationship which we ourselves have been privileged to receive.

The Gospel

I have always found myself reading this prayer as if it is being offered for me. It is offered by our Lord on behalf of his disciples, but to the degree that you and I are his disciples, the prayer is addressed to God on our behalf. I am reminded of two lines of a hymn in Stainer's *Crucifixion:* "Wonder of wonders, O how can it be? Jesus the crucified pleads for me."

I have made your name known to those whom you gave me from the world. Our Lord has made his name known to me through many loving voices and minds.

The words that you gave me I have given to them. His words have been given to me by those who taught me and formed me. This is especially true of anyone of my generation who grew in an educational system that was not in any way secularized and depended a great deal on learning by rote. The words of scripture soaked into one's whole being by sheer repetition and recital.

I have been glorified in them. This statement rather takes one's breath away. Here is Jesus saying that he has been glorified in these disciples, in spite of their pathetic track record. What extraordinary affirmation! Is it then possible that, in spite of my pathetic humanity, our Lord has in some way been glorified in the odd moments of transient worthiness in my life?

Protect them ... that they may be one, as we are one. What can we do when we read this other than to bow our heads in shame? All we can do is to confess our utter failure to be one in the sense that Jesus prays.

I speak these things in the world that they might have my joy. We forget so easily that one of the fruits of the Spirit is joy. What might this mean? Of course, it does not mean that Christians must project a happy face to the world day after day. But consider the fact that it makes a huge difference in modern life to possess a faith. To believe that one is loved, that one is forgiven and accepted, that life is much more than this life, that creation has a meaning and a purpose, that God has entered our human nature in our Lord, has lived it even to the point of dying, and therefore shares the knowledge of our humanity — to possess these things as the basis of one's life makes a tremendous difference. To possess these things as a Christian can sometimes *save us from the evil one* who takes many forms — anxiety, fear, depression, anger, resentment, hopelessness, meaninglessness — all the demons that afflict human lives, robbing them of peace and joy.

Is it possible that our failure to realize these apparently simple things, and to say them to each other, is one of the reasons why the church is unattractive to so many insiders and outsiders alike?

Pentecost

Ezekiel 37:1–14
Psalm 104:25–35, 37b
Romans 8:22–27
John 15:26–27; 16:4b–15

Weavings

These readings tell of the ability of the Spirit of God to energize and transform.

In the first reading, we see the prophet transform a depressed people by recounting his dream of God's transforming actions. In the psalm, we see glorious images of God's Spirit acting through creation. In the second reading, we hear Paul describing how the Spirit of God brings the new to birth in the struggles of both creation and the human spirit. In the gospel passage, we hear our Lord assuring the disciples that there will be a presence in and among them that will energize and transform them.

Reflections

First Reading

We are in the city of Babylon about half a millennium before our Lord's lifetime. We are probably on the outskirts of the city, on the banks of a small tributary of the river Euphrates named the Chebar. Here, in what later ages would call a ghetto, live many of those Israelites who have been brought to Babylon as captives and exiles by the army that has destroyed Jerusalem.

We can guess the mood of the gathering — anger, resentment, homesickness, probably some self-contempt for their own helplessness, and precious little hope. Into this crowd comes Ezekiel. Most people trust him because they know of his reputation back in Jerusalem before the disaster, and they know that he has been faithful to them in this ghastly situation. They are prepared to listen.

I hear Ezekiel telling them that he wants to share a dream he has just had. He uses dreams and symbols and images very powerfully. *The spirit of the Lord ... set me down in the middle of a valley ... full of bones. There were very many ... and they were very dry.* Notice how Ezekiel emphasizes the awfulness of it all: *very many ... very dry.*

Let us try to do now with this dream something like what Ezekiel did with it long ago. Let us hear it speaking to us about our situation as Christians at the present time in Western culture. We, too, seem to be looking at a valley of bones — a dryness and a deadness in contemporary Christian institutional life. To say this is not for a moment to dismiss the church with some lofty and arrogant contempt. Church life has within it much faithfulness, much beauty, many magnificent men and women. But these men and women are faced with an institution that is in very difficult days. There is a general and deep distrust of all institutions, among them religious institutions. In the face of this distrust, the church's energy and self-esteem have dried up. Bones seems to be poking through outer skin.

As in Ezekiel's dream we ask, *can these bones live?* But we need to look carefully at how this question is triggered in his dream. It is God, not Ezekiel, who asks, *can these bones live?* But Ezekiel throws the question right back to God: *O Lord God, you know.*

Now we hear something very significant for us. God says to Ezekiel, *Prophesy to these bones.* In other words, God is rejecting Ezekiel's abrogation of responsibility for answering the question. However, God is not suggesting that Ezekiel must or even can answer it. Maybe nobody can answer it. But God demands of Ezekiel that he respond to the situation with hope, and then wait for what happens. Ezekiel is to assume that the bones can indeed come alive.

This is exactly what God is demanding of us in our doubts and fears about the future of Christian faith and Christian institutions. God is demanding of us that we assume the possibility of new life and act under this assumption. In the language of scripture, it is being demanded of us that we *prophesy to [the] bones.*

Notice the reiteration of the word *will* in the next part of the text. Like many of the great voices of Israel, Ezekiel is daring to speak his hope for the future in certainty of its fulfilment. There is no "may be"; instead there is a repeated "will be." Are we being called to speak with certainty, too?

In the dream there is a response to Ezekiel's decision to risk addressing the bones: *a rattling ... bones came together ... sinews [came] on them ... flesh had come upon them, and skin had covered them.*

But something is still missing. *There was no breath in them.* Here is the ultimate challenge to hope. All the other elements are physical. Breath is of the spirit. In Hebrew, one word names them both. Can Ezekiel dare assume the coming of a new spirit into the bones and sinews and skin?

Ours is the same fear. We can build new structures, new organizations, new walls, new programs, new systems, if we wish to gather the resources. But can we find the source of a revitalized Christian faith? This scripture tells us that with God it is possible, if we are prepared to be faithful to the possibility. *I prophesied as [God] commanded me, and the breath came into them, and they lived, and stood on their feet, a vast multitude.*

Such is this wonderful vision of Ezekiel. We can see him emerging from his mode of dreaming to observe the people in front of him. *I am going to open your graves, and bring you up from your graves, O my people.* Ezekiel can see the deadness and hopelessness in eyes and faces and bodies, just as we can see indifference and discouragement in many places today. To Israel long ago, to Christians today, comes the voice that says,

> *I will put my spirit within you,*
> *And you shall live ...*
> *And ... you shall know*
> *That I, the Lord,*
> *Have spoken*
> *And will act.*

The Psalm

I am about nine years of age. It is Wednesday afternoon choir practice. Through the half-open window, I can see the green of the woods opposite the church. Outside is freedom and play. But suddenly I hear verses of this psalm, and I am transported to a grand different scene. Our piping soprano voices sing, "There go the ships; and there is Leviathan, whom thou has formed to take his pastime therein."

Yes, these are the words I would have sung that day. I was being captured by the language of Miles Coverdale, writing to me from the sixteenth century, telling me of *the great and wide sea, with its living things too many to number, creatures both small and great.* Slightly different language from that of today, but the same images come cascading into my mind. There is the thunder of the ocean, and the booming call of some vast form rising and falling in the waves just beyond the prow of my imaginary ship.

I am using memory to point out the majesty and grand vision of this psalm. To give me images of the work of the creating spirit of God, the psalmist is deliberately thinking in great landscapes and endless vistas. For him God is one who is *[wrapped in] light as with a cloak.* For him God is one who *[makes] the clouds your chariot* and *the winds your messengers.* Paraded before us is the whole vast canvas of creation: *the waters ... the mountains ... the springs ... the beasts of the field ... the birds of the air.* This is a God who makes wine — oceans of it! A God who makes bread — mountains of it! By the power of this God, rises the glory of the sun. And under its golden light, there walks another creature fashioned by God: *People go out to their work and to their labour until the evening.*

Whether one is child or adult, this wonderful song gives us a vision of the creating Spirit of God. *[When] you send forth your Spirit ... they are created.* Yet vast and wonderful and beautiful though this creation be, when *you [God] hide your face ... they are terrified. [When] you take away their breath ... they die and return to their dust.* All this God has to do is *[touch] the mountains and they smoke — [look] on the earth and it trembles.*

No wonder the psalmist intends to *praise my God while I have my being.* A terrifying thought for a choirboy, Leviathan notwithstanding!

Second Reading

Anyone who reads the writings of Paul knows that every now and again his thoughts seem to burst out of normal limitations to pursue some grand idea, some vision that is far-reaching and elusive of precise definition. Yet the thought is so vast and majestic that it reverberates in the mind of the reader. This is such a moment.

In a flash of vision Paul becomes aware of the totality of creation. *We know that the whole creation has been groaning in labour pains until now.* We might consider how extraordinary it is that the human mind can contain within itself the concept of the whole creation, whether expressed in the language of philosophy or theology or astronomy. Yet Paul is also aware of some quality in created things that makes them mysteriously incomplete. Here perhaps is a perception of creation as essentially evolutionary.

Paul intuits that all aspects of creation have in them a kind of pain, an element of struggle. He perceives this in himself, in humanity, and in the natural world. He speaks of this as a *groaning ... inwardly.* All of us know only too well this element of struggle in our lives, both physical and spiritual. And we also see it in the world of nature, suffering under the yoke of human exploitation.

But Paul sees creation and humanity experiencing a particular kind of suffering — *labour pains.* Here is a transforming vision. Paul is prepared to bet that the pain of creation, including the pain of incompletion and striving at the heart of all life, is the pain of new birth in creation and in us.

This is precisely why Paul can continue his train of thought with hope. *If we hope for what we do not see, we wait for it with patience.* Our spiritual struggle, which often fills us with frustration and a sense of unworthiness, is but an opportunity for the Spirit of God to work in us, understanding our shortcomings and compensating for our spiritual poverty. *The Spirit helps us in our weakness.*

The Gospel

Speaking in the shadows of the upper room, knowing that there is very little time left, our Lord is assuring the disciples that there will be a future for the relationship they have shared over the last few years of ministry together.

When the Advocate comes, whom I will send ... he will testify on my behalf. I would risk suggesting that our Lord is saying something like this.

There has been a deep relationship between us now for some time. You have learned from me and committed yourselves to me. This relationship has to end as my life ends. But you will find that our relationship continues in another way. It will continue because you will find that all I have taught you and shown you will be found within you, within your spirit. God, who gave us our relationship with one another, will now give you the fruits of this relationship within you and among you.

Jesus now adds a direction that we need to note carefully in our own lives. *The Spirit ... will testify ... [but] you also are to testify.* Spirituality is not a passive receiving on our part. To be a spiritual being is to be active and intentional about spirituality, giving thought and energy and commitment to its challenges.

Jesus is well aware of the mood around him — sorrow, fear, a sense of being threatened, a rejecting of deep change, puzzlement, even incomprehension. He continues to try to assuage those feelings. We can hear the emphases in his words and tone: *I tell you the truth: it is to your advantage that I go away.*

But the assurance comes with a warning. *When [the Advocate] comes, he will prove the world wrong.* The spirit with which they will be endowed, which will form the church for ages to come, will challenge the cultural and spiritual assumptions of the world they live in. The challenges will at times be costly. In every generation, including our own, some Christian men and women have found this to be painfully true.

Trinity Sunday

Isaiah 6:1–8
Psalm 29
Romans 8:12–17
John 3:1–17

Weavings

Every passage is pointing towards the reality, power, and cease-less working of the Spirit of God.

In the first reading, the Spirit is offered in vision to the shaken Isaiah as he begins a daunting chapter of his life. The psalmist sings of the same Spirit active in the whole of creation. In the second reading, Paul emphasizes how much more there is available to us than merely our own self-centred nature. In the gospel, we listen to a magnificent encounter between Jesus and a person of both great mental ability and great spiritual hunger.

Reflections

First Reading

I have always felt that in this great passage we encounter a twentieth-century viewpoint with startling clarity. Everything here sounds contemporary to us — what is happening in Isaiah's country and the surrounding world at the time, what he is experiencing at this particular stage in his life, and how he is responding to what takes place.

Imagine that you are somewhere between twenty-five and thirty years of age, you have a wife and two young sons, you are reasonably affluent, and you actually have a voice in political life. You live in a small country threatened by the struggles of superpowers. Just at this time the king dies. Very often the death of a prominent public figure affects the way we think about our own lives. This is certainly true in the case of Isaiah. At this point we can observe his experience to see how it speaks to ours.

In the year that King Uzziah died, I saw the Lord. We live at a time when many "kings" — that is, power structures, traditions, assumptions — are dying or changing into something that is not yet fully formed. Perhaps because of this huge transition, a sense of awe and mystery is returning to life. Spirituality is once again respected. Many are, to use Isaiah's term, seeing the Lord.

High and lofty. I feel that, where people today are recapturing a sense of personal faith and divine presence, they are doing so with a heightened view of both — with a faith that is experienced intensely and a view of God that is strongly transcendent.

The hem of his robe filled the temple ... the whole earth is full of his glory. The old idea that God is limited merely to religious issues — more especially institutional religious issues — is passing. All issues and questions are being seen as within the domain of the spiritual.

The pivots on the thresholds shook ... the house filled with smoke. Many people today, their whole world shaken, are filled with a sense of awe and mystery.

In the midst of all this, many feel as if their grip on things is loosening. They lose a sense of meaning, certainty, confidence, and security. They cry out, *I am lost.* Isaiah gives two reasons why he feels at a loss. *I am a man of unclean lips,* he says. In other words, he does not feel worthy. His self-esteem is almost non-existent. But there is a second reason, one we can affirm strongly today. *I live among a people of unclean lips.* He can no longer find support and affirmation from the institutions and structures of the society around him. Many people today no longer feel able to trust structures, whether ecclesiastical, political, educational, or social.

This is the lowest point of Isaiah's experience, and it speaks to the lowest points of our contemporary experience. But suddenly something wonderful and beautiful happens. *One of the seraphs flew to me, holding a live coal that had been taken from the altar.* To put it simply, many people, like Isaiah, experience the gift of grace in some way. Some will receive it in religious terms, some through friends, some by a word or a deed. But all will recognize the grace as coming from beyond themselves, from a transcendent source. With the coming of such grace we feel ourselves to be touched, as Isaiah felt touched by the coal.

Your guilt has departed, the voice says. In other words, it is not that he has been transformed in some magic way, but that his attitude has been changed. The guilt and the sense of unworthiness leave him, and he can respond to what is calling him. Notice the importance of the word *then* in the sentence, *Then I heard the voice of the Lord.* The grace of God has made it possible for him to hear the voice of God calling for his response. The grace of God makes it possible for us to hear the voice of God calling for our response, and makes it possible for our response to be a Yes to God. *I said, Here am I; send me!*

The Psalm

After the Falklands war the English prime minister of that time asked for a service to give thanks for the victory. In his homily the then Archbishop of Canterbury did not so much celebrate a victory as ask forgiveness for the agony of war. In doing so he provoked much anger. However, if a victory psalm had been chosen for that service, it could well have been this psalm.

Ascribe to the Lord glory and strength ... The voice of the Lord is a powerful voice. This song celebrates the fact that the God of those who are singing is not only more powerful than the gods of other nations, but is the ruler of all creation. *The voice of the Lord ... strips the forests bare.* Meanwhile the people are gathered in God's *temple ... all are crying, "Glory!"*

We have difficulty saying this psalm with these meanings. We live in a different time and share a different world. Ironically we have no difficulty identifying with the images used to describe the relationship of God to the natural environment, acknowledging readily that we must bow before a power above our own. However, the image of a temple where all are crying glory is no longer possible for us in an increasingly fragmented society. It is very difficult for us, if not impossible, to think of ourselves as one people, let alone our being the people of one God.

For us the psalm can be a song giving glory to God. We do not see this God as the adversary of other visions of the divine, but as the ultimate reality beyond all such visions. We acknowledge the rule of God over creation, of which we are a part and for which we bear responsibility. We worship this God, knowing that others worship in other ways. Our prayer is that the planet itself may become the temple of God in which humanity cries *"Glory"* in countless tongues, and that this same humanity may come to see itself as a people under God, who make the single prayer, *[May the Lord] give his people the blessing of peace.*

Second Reading

Paul is telling us something he himself has learned by hard experience in his own wrestling with life. He is saying that within us there is not only our own nature, trying to rule us like the tyrant it is, but also another nature, another source of power and grace. This he calls *the Spirit of God.* When he tells us that *we are debtors, not to the flesh,* Paul is referring to something beyond mere physicality. By the term *flesh* he means human nature existing apart from the grace of God.

If we decide that the self is all that exists, then we can feel enslaved by the demands of this self — its needs, desires, and appetites; its sense of having a rightful claim on everything. This is not to say that a sense of the self is evil, but it may become evil if it is allowed to take over our whole being. As Paul says, we then live *with a spirit of slavery.* To know that there is more than the demanding self is to have what Paul calls *a spirit of adoption* — that is, a sense of belonging to someone greater and finer than ourselves. When we become aware of this we find ourselves living in relationship with this source of grace and inspiration as if we were the offspring of one who loves.

We are children of God, says Paul; therefore our lives are endlessly developing and maturing. We are, in Paul's words, *heirs of God.* Christians see in Jesus Christ the example of the perfected Child of God. But just as his relationship with God involved great cost, so may our relationship with the grace beyond ourselves be costly. However, though it may exact a payment from us, it will finally reward us with a deep sense of gain and insight — a sense of victory in our lives.

The Gospel

This is one of the most captivating of all encounters with our Lord in the gospel record. At least it has been so for me, ever since I came to it in school. When a scripture passage has a deep appeal to us, we should ask what it is telling us about ourselves.

Nicodemus is a very powerful person in his society. He is a member of what we might call its inner cabinet. On the surface, he seems to have everything he wishes, yet he also seems to have an unsatisfied inner longing.

He came to Jesus by night. We can only guess why. I suspect that people of Nicodemus's rank did not relish being seen to consult village rabbis. Notice how Nicodemus, used to putting people at ease when they come to him, feels he must do this for Jesus. He begins with a compliment: *Rabbi, we know that you are a teacher who has come from God.* One could assume any rabbi would be pleased to hear this from a prominent and powerful visitor.

But Jesus shows no sign of needing to be complimented or to be set at ease. His very first sentence goes straight to the point. *No one can see the kingdom of God without being born from above.* He says in effect to Nicodemus, "I know you are looking for something in your life. Take my word for it that you have to look towards a source beyond yourself to find it."

Since Nicodemus knows there is truth in what Jesus has just said and feels somehow threatened by it, he indulges in a kind of nervous and sarcastic dismissal of it. *Can anyone be born after having grown old?* The irony is that, at least in the realm of the spirit, it is precisely when we have grown old, or have at least matured, that we most need to be born — not just once, but again and again.

Jesus' bold response must have brought Nicodemus up short. *No one can enter the kingdom of God without being born of water and Spirit.* Jesus is saying again, even more forcibly, that whatever Nicodemus is longing for cannot be drawn merely from his own resources. For one whose whole career has been built from his own resources, this is hard to hear. Nicodemus is an extremely able professional, not attracted to the thought that there is something he cannot achieve of himself.

Notice the two images that Jesus chooses to offer Nicodemus about the kingdom. One is the image of birth, the other that of a *wind that blows where it chooses.* Both are realities that one cannot control. This is not good news to Nicodemus. After all, one does not become a senior government bureaucrat without exercising control over oneself and others. The invitation to turn the deepest levels of his life over to another authority is nothing short of threatening. No wonder that he asks, *How can these things be?* And no wonder that Jesus responds — gently I suspect, but firmly — *Are you a teacher of Israel, and yet you do not understand these things?* I wonder if Jesus is suggesting to Nicodemus that we can be experts in religion as knowledge without becoming rich in spirituality as personal experience. We can feel the force of the accusation ourselves.

By now, the authority in this conversation has passed from Nicodemus to Jesus. Nicodemus, perhaps for the first time for a long time, is listener and learner. What he learns comes in the beauty and truth of what Jesus now tells him. First, Jesus speaks to the Jew in Nicodemus, using the image of the serpent that pointed the Israelites to a source of healing beyond themselves. Second, Jesus offers himself to Nicodemus, providing a source of grace beyond this able man's powerful yet limited human self. *God so loved the world that he gave his only Son, so that everyone who believes in him may not perish but may have eternal life.*